Praise ror *Maurice Richard*

"Charles Foran has skilfully resurrected not only the life of this extraordinary athlete and cultural icon; he has also placed the Rocket in his extraordinary time and place.... A straightforward but engaging account.... Foran succeeds ... in giving us the best account to date of the original Flying Frenchman." —*Winnipeg Free Press*

"From the moment the narrative puck is dropped, Foran uses his power and grace as a novelist to weave readers through moments in Richard's life with accuracy and depth ... a compelling narrative about the life of a gifted athlete, whose singular vision of the sport he loved became for him both a blessing and a curse." —*The Telegraph-Journal*

"Foran is an exemplary writer. He culls the essential from a life and makes it both intriguing and relevant.... Even those not interested in hockey ... will enjoy Foran's chronicle of the game's golden age, his portrait of a society in flux and his sketch of a player who pushed his talent to the limit, and succeeded."

"[Foran] has done a magnificent job of boiling down all the words, film, sound and imaginings of the Rocket and making new sense of this simple man's importance."

—*The Globe and Mail*

"Foran's prose is especially eloquent and is itself worth the price of the book. You don't have to be a hockey fan to like *Maurice Richard.* This is a book for fans of great writing."

—*Canada's History* magazine

"Thankfully, Foran's book is not just another hagiography of the storied Hall of Famer. [He] avoids mythologizing his subject, instead capturing the off-ice melancholy and inner turmoil of hockey's great anti-hero."   —*Quill and Quire*

Praise for the Extraordinary Canadians series

"These books are not definitive biography; rather, they are opportunities to deepen the relationship between Canadians of the past and Canadians of the present. May this dialogue continue, so that today's biographers themselves will be the subject of the next wave of writers." —*The Globe and Mail*

"The concise books are a vivid, 'character-driven patchwork' of modern Canadian history made relevant to modern readers. In other words, no dry academic tomes allowed.... What's compelling about the Extraordinary Canadians series is that it draws you back to some of the original oeuvres—to Anne, to Carr's remarkable paintings or to Glenn Gould's Goldberg Variations." *—Vancouver Sun*

"Marvelous." *—Ottawa Citizen*

"Extraordinary Canadians features snappy, candid, highly personal sketches not meant to be definitive biographies. They are, instead, individual glimpses into the lives of some of the country's most prized achievers." *—London Free Press*

"Gorgeous little books." *—Toronto Star*

"[The] Extraordinary Canadians series, ably edited by John Ralston Saul, is ... appealing because its subject matter is so varied, and the books are all written by people who either knew or took a personal interest in the famous Canadians they're writing about." *—Calgary Herald*

"Entertaining, literary and informative." *—National Post*

"Excellent." —*Winnipeg Free Press*

"The concept of the series is a good one, especially the emphasis on brevity." —*The Walrus*

"Don't be put off by the charming simplicity of format and language of these books. There's a depth and passion to them that is compelling." —*Canada's History* magazine

"A series to collect and cherish. As ambitious a publishing program as has been seen in years, it is a reminder of how good a biography can be." —*The SunTimes* (Owen Sound)

PENGUIN

MAURICE RICHARD

CHARLES FORAN has published ten books, including the multi-award winning *Mordecai: The Life and Times* and *The Last House of Ulster.* He is the great-grandson of an early Stanley Cup trustee and, on his mother's side, a descendant of generations of diehard Montreal Canadiens supporters. He lives in Toronto.

SERIES EDITOR:
John Ralston Saul

Maurice Richard

by CHARLES FORAN

With an Introduction by
John Ralston Saul
SERIES EDITOR

EXTRAORDINARY
CANADIANS

PENGUIN

an imprint of Penguin Canada

Published by the Penguin Group
Penguin Group (Canada)
90 Eglinton Avenue East, Suite 700, Toronto, Ontario, Canada M4P 2Y3

Penguin Group (USA) Inc., 375 Hudson Street, New York, New York 10014, U.S.A.
Penguin Books Ltd, 80 Strand, London WC2R 0RL, England
Penguin Ireland, 25 St Stephen's Green, Dublin 2, Ireland
(a division of Penguin Books Ltd)
Penguin Group (Australia), 707 Collins Street, Melbourne, Victoria 3008, Australia
(a division of Pearson Australia Group Pty Ltd)
Penguin Books India Pvt Ltd, 11 Community Centre, Panchsheel Park,
New Delhi – 110 017, India
Penguin Group (NZ), 67 Apollo Drive, Rosedale, Auckland 0632, New Zealand
(a division of Pearson New Zealand Ltd)
Penguin Books (South Africa) (Pty) Ltd, 24 Sturdee Avenue, Rosebank,
Johannesburg 2196, South Africa

Penguin Books Ltd, Registered Offices: 80 Strand, London WC2R 0RL, England

First published in Penguin hardcover by Penguin Canada, 2011

Published in this edition, 2013

1 2 3 4 5 6 7 8 9 10   (WEB)

Copyright © Charles Foran, 2011
Introduction copyright © John Ralston Saul, 2011

Manufactured in Canada.

LIBRARY AND ARCHIVES CANADA CATALOGUING IN PUBLICATION

Foran, Charles, 1960–
Maurice Richard / Charles Foran.

(Extraordinary Canadians)
Includes bibliographical references.

ISBN 978-0-14-317396-0

1. Richard, Maurice, 1921–2000. 2. Hockey players—Québec (Province)—Biography.
3. Montreal Canadiens (Hockey team)—Biography.
I. Title. II. Series: Extraordinary Canadians

GV848.5.R5F67 2013   796.962092   C2013-900587-0

Visit the Penguin Canada website at www.penguin.ca

Special and corporate bulk purchase rates available; please see
www.penguin.ca/corporatesales or call 1-800-810-3104, ext. 2477.

ALWAYS LEARNING   PEARSON

For my parents,
Dave and Muriel Foran,
and *ma tante* Anna

CONTENTS

John Ralston Saul

How do civilizations imagine themselves? One way is for each of us to look at ourselves through our society's most remarkable figures. I'm not talking about hero worship or political iconography. That is a danger to be avoided at all costs. And yet people in every country do keep on going back to the most important people in their past.

This series of Extraordinary Canadians brings together rebels, reformers, martyrs, writers, painters, thinkers, political leaders. Why? What is it that makes them relevant to us so long after their deaths?

For one thing, their contributions are there before us, like the building blocks of our society. More important than that are their convictions and drive, their sense of what is right and wrong, their willingness to risk all, whether it be their lives, their reputations, or simply being wrong in public. Their ideas, their triumphs and failures, all of these somehow constitute a mirror of our society. We look at these people, all dead, and discover what we have been, but also what we can be. A mirror is an instrument for measuring ourselves. What we see can be both a warning and an encouragement.

These eighteen biographies of twenty key Canadians are centred on the meaning of each of their lives. Each of them is very different, but these are not randomly chosen great figures. Together they produce a grand sweep of the creation of modern Canada, from our first steps as a democracy in 1848 to our questioning of modernity late in the twentieth century.

All of them except one were highly visible on the cutting edge of their day while still in their twenties, thirties, and forties. They were young, driven, curious. An astonishing level of fresh energy surrounded them and still does. We in the twenty-first century talk endlessly of youth, but power today is often controlled by people who fear the sort of risks and innovations embraced by everyone in this series. A number of them were dead—hanged, infected on a battlefield, broken by their exertions—well before middle age. Others hung on into old age, often profoundly dissatisfied with themselves.

Each one of these people has changed you. In some cases you know this already. In others you will discover how through these portraits. They changed the way the world hears music, thinks of war, communicates. They changed how each of us sees what surrounds us, how minorities are treated, how we think of immigrants, how we look after each other, how we imagine ourselves through what are now our stories.

You will notice that many of them were people of the word. Not just the writers. Why? Because civilizations are built around many themes, but they require a shared public language. So Laurier, Bethune, Douglas, Riel, LaFontaine, McClung, Trudeau, Lévesque, Big Bear, even Carr and Gould, were masters of the power of language. Beaverbrook was one of the most powerful newspaper publishers of his day. Countries need action and laws and courage. But civilization is not a collection of prime ministers. Words, words, words—it is around these that civilizations create and imagine themselves.

The authors I have chosen for each subject are not the obvious experts. They are imaginative, questioning minds from among our leading writers and activists. They have, each one of them, a powerful connection to their subject. And in their own lives, each is engaged in building what Canada is now becoming.

That is why a documentary is being filmed around each subject. Images are yet another way to get at each subject and to understand their effect on us.

The one continuous, essential voice of biography since 1961 has been the *Dictionary of Canadian Biography*. But there has not been a project of book-length biographies such as Extraordinary Canadians in a hundred years, not since the Makers of Canada series. And yet every generation understands the past differently, and so sees in the mirror of these remarkable figures somewhat different lessons. As history rolls on, some truths remain the same while others are revealed in a new and unexpected way.

What strikes me again and again is just how dramatically ethical decisions figured in these people's lives. They form the backbone of history and memory. Some of them, Big Bear, for example, or Dumont, or even Lucy Maud Montgomery, thought of themselves as failures by the end of their lives. But the ethical cord that was strung taut through their work has now carried them on to a new meaning and even greater strength, long after their deaths.

Each of these stories is a revelation of the tough choices unusual people must make to find their way. And each of us as readers will find in the desperation of the Chinese revolution, the search for truth in fiction, the political and military dramas, different meanings that strike a personal chord. At first it is that personal emotive link to such figures which draws us in. Then we find they are a key that opens the whole society of their time to us. Then we realize that in that 150-year period many of them knew each other, were friends, opposed each other. Finally, when all these stories are put together, you will see that a whole new debate has been created around Canadian civilization and the shape of our continuous experiment.

Somehow hockey does lie at the core of this Canadian story, not so much as a sport, but as the physical activity by which we measure ourselves. Maurice Richard evokes more than anyone else the game and the way that measurement is conceived. The great player becomes the great symbol—one which he can neither control nor shape to his satisfaction.

This story, which the essayist, novelist and biographer Charles Foran, brings us, is that of a human with whom we can all identify, not because we are great hockey players, but because the game comes alive and with it the social drama of Montreal and Quebec and eventually that of Canada as a whole. Richard's story lies at the heart of the great stage play in which Canadians conceive of themselves.

Maurice Richard

CHAPTER ONE

Nobody

You're either Maurice Richard or you're nobody.
HUBERT AQUIN

He does not skate over the ice so much as impose himself upon it with each pressuring stride. His strokes are economical rather than elegant, commanded by force more than grace. Shoulders square and elbows at ninety degrees, chin up and gaze ahead—superb form, signs of a natural—he manoeuvres the puck side to side on the blade of his stick with the ease of someone stirring milk into coffee. Evident in his carriage, and more so later when he's shown lacing up his skates, is the upper body of a logger or, in another age, a *coureur de bois:* the barrel chest and broad shoulders, tree-trunk arms and thick hands, knuckles permanently swollen. Like many shy men, he does not know what to do with his hands when they aren't fisted for a fight, and dangles them by his side or stuffs them into his pockets. But on ice there is no awkwardness or self-consciousness, only instinct and motor-memory, the focus and control of a predator on the hunt.

Today, however, he skates by himself in the Montreal Forum, ricocheting the puck off the boards and firing into an empty net. Rounding off to launch a rush at half speed, he still outpaces and outmuscles opponents who are—truth be told—phantoms. He is alone on the fabled surface, and alone, by and large, in the stadium that his talent and tenacity once filled, the 16,259 seats empty, the clack of the puck like a distant gunshot. Nor is he in the uniform, the *bleu, blanc et rouge* that he so proudly wore, his number 9 having been retired after he stopped playing. Instead, he is in pants and a sweater—a civilian, an interloper.

It is 1975, and fifty-four-year-old Maurice Richard is back in the Forum for the purposes of a CBC television documentary. The solitary skate, orchestrated by the news program *The Fifth Estate,* speaks to his sense of his current standing. "The fans were a hundred percent behind me because I was French Canadian, and I scored lots of goals," he says of his canonization during the 1940s and '50s as "Saint Maurice," avenger of the injustices suffered by those same French Canadians. "Now the crowd scarcely remembers me." Elsewhere, he admits that he could foresee a time "when nobody recognizes you in the street, when nobody greets you," and adds, "I'm not in a hurry to see that day."

But that day, he believes, has come. Richard can't hide either his bitterness or his confusion at the apparent turn of events. For his part, he hasn't changed at all. He remains handsome, with the same chiselled features and dark eyes, the same hair meticulously groomed. Maybe twenty pounds heavier than when he played, he is still fit and formidable, on ice and off, and is still taciturn and introverted, clumsy with his hands and scarcely more comfortable with his words. He is, matter of fact, recognizably the same intense, nervous young adult who, though skilled at hockey, trained as a machinist during the Depression in the hope of landing a job in the Canadian Pacific Railway yards, just as his father had done, and who then tried three times to enlist in the army to fight Hitler in Europe. The same shy man who married the first and only girl he dated—she asked him out, and persisted—and has stayed a faithful husband to her and a gentle father to their seven children. The same Montrealer who continues to live within a few kilometres of where he grew up in the city's north end; who has always lived among his fans, driving a regular car and owning an ordinary house, eating in everyday restaurants and using a neighbourhood barber; and who once quit an excellent job in Quebec City in part because he didn't like being away from home. The same French-speaker, his Montreal accent underscored by his parents' Gaspé intonations, who learned English only as an adult, and then largely for business, and who rarely travels, except for sun holidays in Florida and fishing and hunting trips up north. Who barely knows the rest of Canada, and is only mildly interested in it, an attitude not challenged by his exposure during his career to just one other city—Toronto, then an ugly, hostile place, inside and out. Who is, truth be told, content with his own town and his own language—with, in effect, his (French) Canada and his (French) Canadians. Who attends church most Sundays, and takes communion; who voted and campaigned for the other famous "Maurice" of his day—*le chef* Maurice Duplessis, the eccentric and autocratic premier who ruled Quebec for twenty years of great darkness.

He is, in short, a man of his generation, abiding by a code of behaviour and comportment learned from his father, and from mentors who had fought in world wars and who wore long wool coats and fedoras. He is also still Saint Maurice, defender and exemplar of the downtrodden French Canadian through both his brilliant play and the righteous violence of his fists.

But in fall 1975, everything about those identities—the

private, the public, the individual, the collective—is being scrutinized. Not found wanting necessarily; simply re-examined in light of the transformations in Quebec since the death of one Maurice—Duplessis, in September 1959— and the retirement from hockey of the other—Richard, in September 1960. So much has changed in those fifteen years of Quiet Revolution, all for the better, but nothing, it seems, has changed about the Rocket, as he continues to be called. He is a living saint in a society that abruptly fled its churches and mothballed its crucifixes. He is a self-defined French Canadian, subservient to various *patrons,* including the malicious *chef,* where people are now Québécois, secular and emancipated, more and more *maîtres chez nous.* He is also, by default, a *habitant* and a *Jean du Pays,* a Chapdelaine and a Plouffe. For some he is an exemplar of the historic, quasi-folkloric "small people," the silent majority—as per the official narrative of recent Quebec history, then being constructed to bolster the nationalist project—who endured bad times from the Anglo conquest in 1759 straight through to *La grande noirceur,* the Great Darkness, as the Duplessis era has been evocatively labelled, on the strength of *tourtières* and *fèves au lard,* folk songs and fiddles, stoicism and Gallic good cheer. For the politicians and technocrats, the professors, writers, and musicians currently forging a new identity for a new society, the "real" Maurice Richard—though he is but a middle-aged man—is, by default, closer to the elderly parent or grandparent figure, if not to the sepia-hued ancestor in period apparel and facial hair.

Even his legendary volatility, his raw-knuckled fisticuffs and brandishing of a hockey stick as weapon, outbursts triggered by the ingrained bigotry of referees and fans elsewhere in the NHL against his kind, feels antiquated. These days, after a flirtation with violent insurrection in the sixties, Quebec is defending and promoting itself through electoral politics, a more sophisticated and probably more successful approach. The separatist Parti Québécois of René Lévesque is twelve months away from being elected as the new government, with a mandate to take the province out of Confederation.

Finally, Maurice Richard is a working-class hero in a society being redefined and redesigned by and for the middle class. Better: he *remains* the same unpolished, prideful, honourable son of a blue-collar Gaspé émigré, largely unaffected by either fame or his own ascendancy, via hockey, to the bourgeoisie. That identity, fine during his playing days, became awkward the moment he retired. Now it is a borderline embarrassment to some.

The CBC *Fifth Estate* documentary confirms, largely by

accident, many of these perceptions. It opens with Richard, dressed in cap and waders, bellowing into a moose horn near a modest hunting lodge he co-owns in northern Quebec. Subsequent images of him motoring across an empty lake in a small boat and sitting alone on a rock nursing a bottle of beer confirm the impression of a solitary man, either outcast or simply positioned outside mainstream culture. His resentment of how he was treated by the Habs management—the beer, we are told, is not a Molson; estranged from the beer family who own the Montreal Canadiens, Richard won't drink the brand, and didn't allow it to be served in the tavern he once owned—spills over into a larger anger about money. "I guess I was born twenty years too early," he says of reports of the ageless Gordie Howe, his great on-ice rival in the 1950s, then still playing professionally for a six-figure salary alongside his own two sons. Rocket Richard, the host notes, never earned more than $20,000 with the Canadiens—a good wage, but hardly commensurate with the money he brought into the team's coffers. Richard himself adds that his performances on ice generated the kinds of profits NHL owners can only dream of these days, given the rise in player salaries since his retirement.

Though it is not reported on television, Maurice Richard had requested an appearance fee from *The Fifth Estate*. The producers, braced for a sky-high sum—$5000 wouldn't have been unthinkable—almost winced at the figure his agent proposed: $200. Though he no longer endorses products by the dozen, as he did in his prime, he still lends his name and face to local plumbing and electricity companies. He also sells fishing tackle, which he makes himself in his basement, carefully signing each lure, and does the odd paid appearance at banquets—for, presumably, fees in the $200 range.

Another uneasy truth emerges from the documentary. While once quietly sartorial—the pressed suits and cuff-linked shirts, long coats and hats, and polished black shoes worn by hockey players back in the day—and still attentive to his appearance, Richard has never been Jean Béliveau, his gracious, well-spoken successor as team captain and lately as a vice-president of the Habs, a man so naturally patrician his name will eventually come up as a possible governor general of Canada. He isn't Guy Lafleur either, the dashing, crowd-pleasing successor to Béliveau, a heartthrob and hipster just right for the cocky 1970s. His shyness and deep reserve, a kindly but brooding nature, never made him a natural or effective leader away from the rink. Now, with the force of his on-ice character a fading memory, he is permanently diminished, a regular guy who was once something bigger, or even someone else.

"The man we were looking for," the CBC reporter tells the rest of Canada, "was Maurice Richard the folk hero, the saint; we wanted the fire and flash that made the Rocket an idol to millions. What we found instead was a quiet, friendly fifty-four-year-old who was retired firmly if not quite happily."

Richard likely concurs with this verdict. He isn't unaware of his own nature, and how it is factoring into the direction his post-hockey life is taking. But he is also probably of the view that his character is beyond being controlled, let alone made over. He is who he is and, maybe more importantly, he lives where he lives. It does not matter that in 1955 he was invited onto the popular American variety program *Toast of the Town,* hosted by Ed Sullivan, alongside golfer Ben Hogan and boxers Joe Louis and Jack Dempsey, and called "Canada's most famous athlete." It does not matter that he was among the inaugural recipients of the Order of Canada upon its creation in 1967, or that he is revered across the country and has been for decades. Even the should-be-pleasing truth that the Montreal Canadiens squads he led were the team of choice for hockey fans in Pincher Creek, Alberta, and Revelstoke, British Columbia, as well as those in Rimouski and Lac-Saint-Jean, is immaterial. In 1975, Rocket Richard is locked into a conversation with Quebec, and Quebec only.

He is also locked *into* the conversation Quebec is having with itself, his passive role that of a living (if still happily mute) symbol. Lately out of fashion, Richard the symbol is finding utility in the nationalist project. Quebec nationalism, grounded in a nineteenth-century model of the nation-state, requires foundation myths, and Rocket Richard can provide a stirring, motivational one. The man may be incapable of transformation, but the icon is malleable. There is much to be made of that grainy footage of hockey heroics. There is much to be made, once again, of the ferocity he displayed inside the Forum and, less so, the grave dignity he showed outside it.

Biographies, songs, and plays are starting to see in the story of Maurice "Rocket" Richard a larger struggle from darkness into light, with the solitary hero fighting for a cause, a language, even for a nation. Some takes on him are hagiographic, others critical; some slot him into a Quebec nationalist narrative while one, by a Toronto playwright writing in English, aligns his symbolic import with forces larger and more mysterious.

Examples abound. There is the 1976 biography *Maurice Richard: L'idole d'un peuple* by Jean-Marie Pellerin. "And Maurice, who understood, who lived, who incarnated the aspirations of his people, yes, say it, of his people, who would not stop until he reached the summit," swoons the preface. "By his grandeur, by his nobility, by his pride, Maurice Richard helped everyone find strength. He permitted a nation to recover its pride and claim its place in the sun."

Then there's the 1977 song "Essaye donc pas" by nationalist folk singer Paul Piché:

Essaye donc pas
d'être aussi bon
dans tes chansons
qu'Maurice Richard
Maurice Richard
y'tait trop fort
au hockey
pour t'essayer.

Piché sings:

Don't even try
to be as good
with your songs
as Maurice Richard.
Maurice Richard
he was too good

at hockey

for you to even try.

Or the play, likewise from 1976, *Un pays dont la devise est je m'oublie* (A Country Whose Motto Is I Forget) by Jean-Claude Germain. His Rocket Richard speaks "authentic" *joual.* "Maybe it's 'cause I never went to school ... but for me there's one thing I just don't get in all those lessons of theirs!" runs a literal translation. "Sometimes, it's like them educated people and me ... we don't live in the same country. They talk better than me! They know more than me! But I bet they gave up tryin' to score long ago!"

Finally, there's the 1977 play *Les Canadiens* by Toronto author Rick Salutin. In it, a mother explains who the great Richard is, her monologue bilingual and imbued with the rhythms of Catholic prayer:

Dieux du Forum,

Forum Gods!

Oh you, gloire à toi, Maurice.

Oh Rocket, aux pieds longs,

Tu es le centre de la passion

Qui régénère notre nation

And you showed us the way and a light and a life.

Maurice Richard is probably unaware of much of the cultural activity lately swirling around his image and career. Unlike during his ascent to legend as a player in the 1940s and '50s, these appropriations aren't occurring in venues he is familiar with, that he can relate to: inside rinks and on *La soirée du hockey* broadcasts, on radio call-in shows and in the sports pages of tabloids. Instead he is being discussed in books and magazines, in the lyrics of protest songs and on the stages of theatres. Motives are being attributed to his actions and words put into his mouth by people who had little to do with his actual professional life, his actual on- and off-ice battles, with his French Canada. People whose agendas and intentions are strange, and possibly—*possibly*, for how can one tell what those clever young poets and playwrights are trying to say?—hostile. Or so, at least, it may feel to him.

Even if Richard is aware of these contemporary takes on him, he can't respond to them. From the age of twenty-three onwards, he was an athlete whose actions were credited with larger implications. His play bore the expectations and dreams of people very close to him, people he knew and understood: fans gathering outside the barbershop where he had his hair trimmed before games and in the restaurants where he ate with his family, in the foyer after mass at his parish church. That attention and scrutiny was a burden—small at the start of his career, monstrous by the middle of it, and oddly comforting toward the end—that he could take on, albeit with constant anxiety and deepening frailty. All he had to do back then was play hockey, something he was built for and was good at; all he had to say could be communicated on ice, the eloquence unmistakable. Like many great athletes, their brilliance or even genius aligned to the kind of bodily perfection reserved for early and early-middle adulthood, his after-career has been, inevitably, a long anticlimax. Losing that form of expression leaves some athletes effectively mute for the rest of their lives, no matter how well-honed their stories of the good old days. For the taciturn Richard, the silence is now layered; no longer able to express himself through his body, he remains inarticulate, language more a barrier than an aid to communication.

For a proud man, all this must be galling. It's almost as though he is already dead, a statue covered in pigeon dung or a street with his name on it. (By fall 1975 the Maurice Richard Arena already existed in East Montreal; it would host Olympic events the next summer.) That, or else he should be long gone, forefather to the nation who has fallen in brave battle or even—with apologies to the church-closing, crucifix-mothballing new Quebec—who has died,

Dieu nous bénisse, for unspecified earlier sins. It would be a better narrative, a stronger story, for the Rocket and for Quebec alike. It would certainly be less discomfiting than these snippets of the still-living, still-silent Maurice Richard, the everyman sitting on a rock stewing about the Molson family or making fishing lures in his basement.

Back in 1962, in the early days of the *la Révolution tranquille,* the novelist and melancholy separatist Hubert Aquin went public with his own bitterness about being a French-Canadian intellectual by declaring that in Quebec you were a nobody unless you *were* Maurice Richard. Aquin's arresting point was that French Canadians should not need a fearsome black-eyed hockey warrior to make their aspirations known in Ottawa or Toronto; the rest of Canada should naturally be interested in, and respectful of, Quebec's culture and language. Instead, it takes a mythic athlete who once triggered an actual riot in the streets of Montreal to draw attention to an otherwise anonymous—to the rest of the nation—minority. Fifteen years later, shortly after the standing, or utility, of Rocket Richard had bottomed out, dismissed as too tradition-bound and pre-emancipated, Hubert Aquin committed suicide on the grounds of a convent school in Montreal. Had Richard known about Aquin's remark, and met the author shortly before he took his life—more improbabilities, given his nature—he might have overcome his native reticence enough to ask the novelist a question, one that might have soothed Aquin's hurt soul: What does it mean for, if not Quebec, then for one French Canadian, if even Maurice Richard feels like a nobody too?

CHAPTER TWO

A Small People

> We are not a small people, we are maybe something
> of a great people.
> RENÉ LÉVESQUE

They came from the countryside to the cities, fleeing not so much the hardships of farming up in the Saguenay or out on the Gaspé, in the Beauce or the Gatineaus, as the prospect of more of the same for their offspring. Six-month winters these French Canadians could abide. Village life they liked, the intimacy and familiarity, the one shop and one-room school, the one church with the one priest. They prayed and ate, sang and danced together; their many children married each other and had many more. If they were poor it wasn't so bad, unless the frosts came early or someone took seriously ill and a family had to seek help from neighbours and the church. Or until letters started arriving from those exiled sons and daughters who had migrated to Quebec City and Montreal, with reports of the vast riches they were observing in Westmount and Outremont, along with the small amounts of cash they were sending back.

Onésime Richard left the Gaspé during World War I. For nearly two centuries the Richards had eked out livings on the windswept Magdalene Islands in the Gulf of Saint Lawrence. Onésime's father, Henri, had migrated onto the mainland, settling in Amqui, a town in the wooded Matapédia valley in the belly of the peninsula. Bypassing Quebec City, Henri's second son rode the train to Montreal, hoping that some informal training as a carpenter would land him a skilled position. If not, there were bridges being built and a busy port, all requiring strong young men willing to work ten-hour days and six-day weeks. Onésime brought with him the character of the hardscrabble region that been home for eight generations of Richards. Gaspesians were known for their pride, stubbornness, and hard work, and though isolated by language, most had grown up in the company of equally working-class anglophones along the New Brunswick border. Another native of the peninsula, Alice Laramée, made her separate way to the city at around the same time, dreaming of a position as a domestic or shop assistant. Sprawling Montreal—also an island in the Saint Lawrence, though it did not feel embraced by water—overwhelmed country people, until they learned to claim some small patch as their own. East Montreal or St. Henri was where many lived, and, homesick for their kind, they gathered in a park on Notre-Dame Street on Sundays for picnics. Severe, silent Onésime Richard, dark-eyed and long-faced, with thin lips that struggled to form a smile, met petite, shy Alice Laramée, her face rounder but her hair and eyes likewise dark, at one such sociable. The two nineteen-year-olds courted for a few months before marrying in October 1920 in a city church. Fellow exiles attended the modest ceremony, but almost no family: the Gaspé was two days by train, and at least two worlds by connection, from this new life.

There was little question about where in Montreal the couple would settle. Canada's largest urban centre had its divides, and they were as evident as Mount Royal itself, the stubby mountain centring the island. Tradition had it that the minority English resided on one side—on and around the "west" mount, in impossibly wealthy Westmount and more middle-class Notre-Dame-de-Grâce (NDG) next door—and the majority French on the other, with Outremont ("Beyond the Mountain") housing the especially affluent along its slope. The rest of the French population were spread farther east over the Plateau and the thinning tip of the island. The reality was more complex, with poor

French also living down toward the seaway in St. Henri and Verdun, alongside the working-class Irish and Scots of Griffintown and Pointe-Saint-Charles. The bursting Jewish ghetto, its lingua franca a blend of Yiddish and accented English, had lately drifted north of Sherbrooke to the streets around St. Lawrence Boulevard, and Italians and Greeks were pouring off the boats from the upheaval of the recently ended war. Some seven hundred thousand people called the island of Montreal home in 1921, rendering it a distinctly New World urban stew of languages and identities, all in lively competition for linguistic and political space.

Overall, of course, the province of Quebec was predominantly French. Even on the island, six in ten Montrealers, including a disproportionate number of the poor, spoke it as their native tongue. Half of those again, including Onésime and Alice Richard, possessed no other. English may have been overrepresented in street and commercial signs, and most business was conducted in the language, but the city's street music was largely *en français*.

So was its very own drone: the murmur of chanted prayers, at mass or in schools or during a million bedside Angelus devotions, rosary beads clacking in rhythm. Imposing stone churches and severe grey nunneries hunkered like military installations along virtually every major thoroughfare. As Mark Twain had noted forty years earlier during his visit to Montreal, you couldn't throw a brick without hitting a church window. It was certainly hard to walk a block without being presented with additional evidence of the predominance, and potency, of Catholicism. The Church owned land in the city the way royalty owned land in England, and it owned, almost literally, its large, and largely French, flock of penitent, devoted adherents, a congregation schooled in obedience and the sufferings of Jesus Christ for all our sins. (The great exception, Saint Patrick's Cathedral, was built by and for the equally fervent Irish Catholics.) With "their" Church and faith so dominant, and their language the daily music and daily prayer alike, the French surely owned Montreal.

If they didn't—and truth was, the city was ruled by a small autocracy and run by Church dictates and Anglo and French money equally—it was only because French Canadians weren't yet aware of their own size. Told they were a "small people," a helpless minority cast adrift by history in a vast sea of North American difference, they denied what their own eyes and ears reported. They had also been taught that ultimate reward for the faithful lay not in this life, but in the life everlasting. Catholicism preached philosophical quietude, a convenient forbearance for those wishing to remain in political and economic charge.

Onésime and Alice rented a small house on Mentana Street, near Lafontaine Park in the east end. He found jobs as a carpenter; she got pregnant. A decade before the Depression, unemployment rates around the city hovered at 25 percent. Many men worked for day wages, the pay low and the conditions harsh, bringing their packet back to apartments sparse of furniture and heated by a single coal stove. Children stuffed the two or three rooms, with space sometimes made for grandparents, lately relocated from the countryside as well, once they grew too infirm to work the land. Illness could wipe out any savings in a morning—a national health plan was fifteen years, and much misery, away—and no welfare scheme stood between joblessness and a catastrophic fall. Nor were there any pensions for those old people, *nos vieux.* Survival was blunt: earn a salary—and so make the rent and pay the coal and icemen, the grocer who kept a tab, the doctor who accepted only cash—or else. Even before 1929, Montrealers living in decent districts were accustomed to watching neighbours endure the trauma of eviction, their threadbare belongings tossed onto the flat of a rented cart. They could only bless themselves in thanks—*au Nom du Père,* in the Name of the

Father, the Son, and the Holy Spirit—that it wasn't them piling on the suitcases and bags for the slow horse ride downscale to the "slums" of St. Henri, where rents were cheaper and apartments shoddier still.

Joseph Henri Maurice was born on August 4, 1921, in that Gaspé household on Mentana Street. He was a healthy baby, with clear eyes and a full head of hair. Onésime got hired not long after as a *menuisier*, a woodworker, by the Canadian Pacific Railway, and was assigned to their massive Angus Yards off Iberville. The yards, which had lately produced artillery shells for the war effort, manufactured locomotives and freight cars, along with passenger cars with wood interiors. For diligent, polite Onésime it was a real job, with security and modest benefits. Working at the Angus Yards made staying in the area, or moving even farther east, logical. But Gaspé exiles had recently found a spot that came close to replicating the landscape of their beloved home. The village of Bordeaux, north of the downtown and tucked along the Rivière des Prairies, the narrow river separating the islands of Montreal and Laval, had moving water and a railway bridge, fields, and even patches of woods. Along Gouin Boulevard were the kinds of traditional homes, with their mansard roofs and wooden casement windows, that dotted similar small towns throughout the province. Passing by those houses were the same priests in black soutanes and nuns in habits, en route between the nearby hospital and any one of a half-dozen churches. There were also schools, shops, and parks; plus, less remarked, a forbidding octagonal building off Gouin: Bordeaux Prison, opened in 1912, where men were hanged for their crimes.

Best of all, between the village and the next major street to the south, Jean Talon Boulevard, sprawled five miles of fields. Bordeaux wasn't the country, but it wasn't the city either, and Gaspé exiles felt more at ease there. Railway tracks ran up along the eastern fringe, heading north into the Laurentians or northeast along the shore of the Saint Lawrence. The lonely sound of the train, especially at night, reminded the Gaspesians of their homes a hundred, or five hundred miles, away.

In Bordeaux the "small people" could shop, pray, skate, and drink, in French, and still be in cosmopolitan Montreal. "Angus Yards" and the "Canadian Pacific Railway" may have been English names, like the names of most streets and parks and the words on most signs throughout the city, but in Bordeaux, isolated from *les Anglais,* the majority of whom had no idea the village even existed, the parks were called *des bataliers* and the streets had names like Gouin, Viel, and Desenclaves.

Or the grand-sounding Bois-de-Boulogne Avenue, the ordinary street where Onésime, having saved up for years, purchased land and used weekends and holidays to build a tidy three-storey house. Maurice was almost four, and his baby sister Georgette a toddler, when their parents packed their furniture and belongings on the backs of flatbed trucks for the move. Number 1117 Bois-de-Boulogne had neighbours to the north, east, and west, but not the south. For years it was the final house on the street, affording views of those fields and of the west slope of Mount Royal with its unfinished but already astonishing dome of Saint Joseph's Oratory, the basilica where men, women, and children were reportedly healed of their ailments by the miraculous intervention of Brother André. While Bordeaux was not close to the Angus Yards, Onésime, an athletic man fond of softball and hockey and known for his competitive streak, rode his bike each morning to the top of the Bordeaux-Montreal North tramline, opened the same year his first son was born. From there he would travel down to Jean Talon, then transfer streetcars to the east end. An hour each direction, in all weather.

Maurice was four when his father bought him skates. Though Onésime used buckets of water to flood a small rink in the yard adjacent to the house, it was scarcely needed.

Much of Bordeaux was a skating surface from November until April. The river, flooded sections of parks, even the streets themselves, all turned to glass. Runners replaced wheels on the carts in winter, helping to pack down the snow. Banks of snow, high as street signs, were likewise hardened, and useful as boards. Skating at four, by five or six the eldest Richard child—he had another sister now, Marguerite—was playing shinny on those surfaces, including his favourite: out on the river, near the railway bridge, the rink vast and the ice the silvery sheen of a new nickel. A fifteen-minute walk, or a five-minute skate, brought the boy there. It was always cold and often windy, and from the start he was fast, with quick, choppy strides. He pushed naturally back against the wind, never minding the bite pinking his cheeks and stinging his eyes. Outdoor shinny, minus equipment or uniforms, was the only kind of hockey Maurice played until he was fourteen. "Hog" was the popular game. It consisted of holding onto the puck while the other skaters tried to take it from you. Strength and balance, stickhandling and skating—holding on to the puck for a minute meant racing all over the ice—were needed to succeed at Hog.

Hockey was primordial across Quebec, and for most kids it was played outdoors, where its nature, as a response to winter, a physical engagement between a landscape and its inhabitants, was that much more vital. A "rink," designated by snowbanks and maybe stones as goalposts, was a fraction of the surface one skated upon. Around it loomed more ice and more snow, along with walls of trees and a vaulting sky. At night, the surfaces dimly, irregularly lit by nearby street lamps, the sky now collapsed or a partial dome of high, aloof stars, the experience was dreamlike: the *shhh* of blades over the surface, sticks clacking against each other. To skate fast and hard, pushing into that rasping wind, inhaling air so crisp the lungs first rejected it, was to be a wild, free creature, unafraid of the fierce climate—leaning into it, almost, anxious to be part of the land.

Professional hockey put wooden boards around the rink and steel pipes and meshing for the net. It put a roof on winter. The sport, evolved from European stick-and-ball pastimes on slippery frozen rivers and the warlike Aboriginal game of lacrosse, was still figuring itself out. (The word *hockey* derives either from "hoquet," French for a shepherd's staff, or "hoghee," Iroquois for a tree branch.) The first proper game, with some of the rules Maurice Richard played by in the early 1930s, took place in 1875 at Victoria Skating Rink, below St. Catherine Street. A rugby player named James Creighton, wanting to keep in shape in the off-season, devised a set of rules, created two teams of ten, and designated a smaller surface on the vast Victoria rink—eighty-five feet by two hundred—as the arena of play. All ten men skated at once, for the entire game; passes had to be lateral, as in rugby; and the goalie, wearing the same equipment as anyone else—the hard rubber puck stayed on the ice—stood between two pipes, with a judge positioned, improbably, behind him, ready to raise a white hankie when the puck passed in between. The sticks, supplied to both sides by Creighton, were made by Mi'kmaq craftsmen in Nova Scotia.

In the intervening thirty years, rules had evolved and teams, even leagues, had come and gone, with Montreal remaining the centre of the new sport, and its laboratory. With the advent in 1918 of the National Hockey League, its headquarters in the downtown, the city became the literal capital. Since 1909 Montreal had hosted two professional teams: the Wanderers, later the Maroons, for English players and fans, and the Canadiens, increasingly for the huge, mostly untapped French market. French Canadians, believing hockey to be the purview of mostly well-heeled Scottish and English gentlemen, didn't take to it until the 1890s. But once they did, a distinct French style of play, characterized by better skating, more speed, and less rugby-derived contact, emerged. The Canadiens floundered as a franchise until they finally won the Stanley Cup—a challenge cup that had already existed for a quarter-century—in 1924, when Maurice was three. That squad comprised two anglophone stars, Joe Malone and Howie Morenz, but more skaters with names like Léo Dandurand, Aurèle Joliat, Pit Lepine, Edouard Dufour, and goalie Georges Vezina. These were *les Canadiens* or *les Habitants—les/*the *Habs* already—indicated by the insignia on their uniforms: a C intersecting with an H. No M for Montreal: the team represented all French Canadians everywhere; the people of Lac-Saint-Jean and Rimouski, Trois-Pistoles and Trois-Rivières.

Bordeaux was a wonderful place to grow up. Everything was close by, familiar, cozy. *Bonjour, monsieur le prêtre,* Maurice would say to the priest, walking or skating to the rink a block from the house; shopkeepers would likewise be *Monsieur Guindon* and *Madame Fouchette*. He was the quiet eldest boy of Onésime, the one who was always on skates, always playing, and who in summer was known to jump off the railway bridge into the river. But in 1930 his skilled, hardworking father, a non-drinker devoted to his growing family, was laid off. The reality of the Depression, already evident across the city in the piles of furniture outside the apartments of evicted tenants and crowds of men waiting at factory gates, the lineups outside soup kitchens and the shelters set up by the Church, invaded their village idyll. One in three men was now out of work, and few of those had savings to fall back on. The government, faced with actual starvation in the more and more crowded cities, introduced *secours direct*, or direct assistance, a program that provided food coupons for the poor. The Richards had need of them, but Onésime couldn't show his face in the local grocer when others were still paying their bills with cash. Maurice collected the groceries instead, waiting until those with real money were served first. Later, he ran errands and caddied at a golf course in nearby Ahuntsic, all to contribute pennies and dimes. He was the first-born, the keen but quiet observer of his father's grave dignity and decorum, as well as his muffled rages and bitterness. When the Depression started there were five children for Alice Richard to raise: in addition to Maurice, Georgette, and Marguerite, there was now a girl baptized Rollande and a boy called René. By the middle of the decade three more sons would be born: Jacques, Henri, and Claude.

Eight children was a normal family size for French Canadians. The Richards, regulars at mass at nearby Saint Joseph's, didn't need to consciously heed the Church's *la revanche des berceaux* ("revenge of the cradles") policy intended to counter the dilution of "pure" Quebec by the arrival of foreigners. Neither did they have to listen closely to the priest's message, louder now that times were especially tough, about the decadence of cities and how the "real" Quebec lay in the very towns and countryside many had fled for Montreal and its jobs. These instructions and allegiances were transmitted as naturally as prayers learned first in school, then at church, then kneeling by the bed each evening. In 1936 Maurice Duplessis was elected premier. As the leading exponent of the populist social conservatism that would so profoundly shape Quebec over the next three decades, he believed that secret forces hostile to the "small people" had too long controlled the province, and had even brought on the global financial crisis. Fiercely anti-Communist and sympathetic to fascism, the premier envisioned a French Canada for *les habitants*—knowing their place, and happy with it.

By the time Henri was born in 1936, Onésime had his job back, and the worst of the Depression had passed. Maurice had lately been recruited by the Bordeaux parish team to play against rival parishes in the north end. These kids were older than he was, but he was soon dominant, relentless and impossible to get off the puck. The fifteen-year-old was recruited again by a team in the juvenile division playing out of Lafontaine Park, back near where he was born. That meant citywide competition, with the skill level accordingly higher. In his first game in the city league Maurice Richard scored six goals; in the last of his three seasons he was responsible for all but eleven of his team's 144 goals. He was fierce and driven and, though skinny, had powerful arms and legs and, at five foot ten, good height. (Howie Morenz was five-seven, Aurèle Joliat just five-three.) His coach thought he could make the juniors, even the pros, if he toughened up.

In hockey, a sport with an already singular tolerance for fisticuffs, that meant learning how to fight. The coach sent Richard for boxing lessons at a gym operated by a local professional fighter. His instincts weren't wrong; within a year, the teenager was fighting in Golden Gloves competitions around Montreal. Maurice, it turned out, had quick fists, along with a notably short fuse. In no time he became easy to provoke into a fight on the ice but hard to beat. By seventeen, having dropped out of high school to help generate income for the family, he was on the roster for three different teams, including one at the technical school where he was now training as a machinist. He used a false last name to get around regulations in one league, and routinely played four, five games a week, with two on Saturday and, if his father suggested it, some practice skating and shooting after mass on Sundays. A machinist, Onésime agreed, was a good trade: with the economy recovering and another war in Europe now likely, factories needed men to make cars, trucks, tractors, and airplanes. But he also knew his boy had real talent for hockey. He might just make it to the NHL.

Though he still lived at home, sharing a room with two brothers, Maurice spent less and less time in Bordeaux. Taking the St. Lawrence streetcar from its terminus a mile from Bois-de-Boulogne Avenue meant riding a bike, as his father did, balancing hockey gear and stick, and then transferring at Mont Royal over to Lafontaine Park. He slowly learned about the larger city that was his hometown. But if the slum of St. Henri was a neighbourhood he was familiar with, he knew nothing at all of grand Westmount, and the Jewish ghetto was little more than a strange Mitteleuropa full of men in black coats, hats, and side curls, a sight he glimpsed only from inside the St. Lawrence streetcar. He would not step foot inside the Montreal Forum, home to the Canadiens, until the day he received his tryout with the team, and even at age eighteen may have only admired the building once or twice from the street. It was located in the west end of the downtown, at Atwater and St. Catherine. That was English-speaking Montreal, a place, a people, a

Canada, as alien to him as New York or London. Nor could he have approached an Anglo Montrealer, or a Jew, and said more than hello. Like his parents, like his siblings and most of his teammates, Maurice spoke only French.

One of his Bordeaux teammates was George Norchet. His father was a butcher, and his parents encouraged their son to invite the players back to their house after games for sandwiches and soft drinks. George had a younger sister, Lucille, who, though not quite fourteen, decided that the awkward, nearly mute Maurice Richard was the boy for her. He was seventeen, and decidedly rough-hewn: minimal social skills, his hands already dangling uselessly, and with the clothes and bad teeth of someone raised poor. But he was also polite, thanks to his father, and had eyes so dark and sad they betrayed a sensitive soul. She was petite and pretty, a vivacious redhead with social skills to compensate for his lack thereof and a certainty that he would make a good husband and even father—never mind that he rarely said a word to her, or anyone else. They began a chaste courtship, each the other's first romance, with her parents worried less about his prospects than their youth. Lucille was soon Maurice's closest friend as well as his fiancée.

Maurice Richard had still only ever heard the Canadiens play on the radio, and seen sketches and photos of players in the newspapers, when a bizarre accident demonstrated how much hockey meant to Montreal. Nineteen-twenties hero Howie Morenz, now thirty-four, was brought back to the Habs after two seasons elsewhere. The "Stratford Streak," as the native of southern Ontario was called, remained hugely popular with French and English fans equally. He was once more paired on a line with the elderly Aurèle Joliat, the same duo that had led the Canadiens to the Stanley Cup in 1924, and again in 1930 and '31. (The crosstown rival Maroons had won three Cups during that period.) Box office sales were down by half from the great years—the Depression had made even a cheap ticket too steep—and the franchise needed a spark. The return of Howie Morenz provided it. More than twelve thousand attended a Forum game early in January 1937, even though the arena had only nine thousand seats. But on January 28, Morenz slid into the end boards after catching his skate blade in a crack between two planks of wood, and then was piled into by a defenceman. His leg snapped, breaking in four places between the ankle and the knee, and he was put in a cast and held in traction. Hospitalized for six weeks, Morenz suffered some kind of nervous breakdown and, drinking heavily in his room, suffered a fatal heart attack. On March 11 his funeral was held at the Forum. Fans, very soon of the collective opinion that

Howie Morenz, knowing his career with the Habs was now ended, had died of a broken heart, lined up for hours to view his body.

A devastated Joliet retired a year later, and the Habs, designed to embody the aspirations and passions of French Canadians, went into a tailspin, with empty stands, losing seasons, and fewer and fewer players whose family names could speak to that constituency. So much so that, two years later—a tumultuous two years, admittedly, in which a new European war broke out—there was talk of suspending play for a season, or even of folding the franchise. The Montreal Canadiens needed to find a new French-Canadian star, one who would burn bright and long, and they needed to find him fast.

CHAPTER THREE

La Guerre, Yes Sir!

We will have our French state. And we will have a French
country, a country that will carry its soul on its face.
ABBÉ GROULX, 1937

Among the 126 players invited to the Verdun Maple Leafs
training camp in fall 1939 was the apprentice machinist
Maurice Richard. In the summer he had worked for a company that manufactured plumbing supplies, riding his bike
several kilometres each way in the mornings and evenings.
Now he was getting shifts near his father at the CPR's Angus
Yards, and attending tryouts for the Verdun Juniors, as they
were better known, in the evenings. Though he secured the
final spot on the squad, the eighteen-year-old didn't play
much during the season, riding the bench with the other
rookies. His coach liked him enough to insist he get his teeth
fixed—the dentist pulled most out, making a false set—
while also encouraging the left winger to continue with boxing lessons. Hockey at this level wasn't for boys or soft young

men; the game was already tough, and if you couldn't stop an explosive forward, you felled him, often using your stick as an axe. That, or you challenged him to a fight, scared him, made him wish he was back among the juvenile teams skating on Lafontaine Park. Sure enough, Maurice, training for a Golden Gloves tournament, took a punch in the nose, breaking it but not damaging the new teeth, which he had wisely removed beforehand. Only in the playoffs did he manage some ice time, scoring seven goals in as many games. He rode a bus into Ontario for a game in the town of Oshawa, outside Toronto—his first glimpse of the other "Canada," the second part of his designation as a "French Canadian." His playoff numbers got him invited in the summer of 1940 to the team's affiliated squad in the Quebec Senior Hockey League. That marked another rung up the tall ladder to the pros.

Much had changed around the teenager that winter. On September 1, 1939, Adolf Hitler invaded Poland, triggering declarations of war on Germany by Great Britain, France, and Canada. Mandatory military service existed in England, but Prime Minister Mackenzie King assured Canadians that he could not foresee any similar need. Regardless, many French Quebecers declared pre-emptively that they had no interest in fighting English Canada's conflict in Europe.

These included provincial politicians deciding the war was not the business of their kind, the Church dissuading young men from joining for fear the "small people" would not survive the loss of its youth, and even the colourful mayor of Montreal, Camillien Houde, expressing the view that he saw no reason why French Canadians, long-suffering and much humiliated, would want to die for England. In the two years since the historian and priest Abbé Lionel Groulx had shocked many, including Premier Duplessis, by announcing a nationalist agenda from the pulpit of the second-ever Congrès de la langue française in Quebec City, a populist nationalism had come to the fore in Quebec. Duplessis himself, who wanted no part in Groulx's "French nation," propagated a version of it, as did Mayor Houde. The anti-war Duplessis, however, was voted out of office in the fall, thanks to an efficient campaign by the Liberal Adélard Godbout. Houde, meanwhile, accused the prime minister of lying about conscription and was interned for five years in New Brunswick for his disloyalty.

But young men around Montreal, whether French, English, Jewish, Italian, or Greek, were signing up to serve in Europe, and the city was being converted into an enormous armament-manufacturing centre. Posters showed machinists at their lathes helping build fighter planes, and working at the Angus Yards brought Maurice Richard into contact with thoughts and feelings about the war effort far from the rhetoric of politicians and clerics, for whom even a global conflagration was fodder for local posturing. Godbout's government also sided with many of Mackenzie King's policies on the war, taking on the Catholic Church by granting voting rights for women (1940) and introducing compulsory education for children up to the age of fourteen (1943). Wartime Quebec, especially the island of Montreal, was progressive, and not so evidently under the thumb of Church-driven social conservatism and populist national-ism, the powerful, pinching forces of both the recent past and the pending future. Maurice Richard, who had no par-ticular interest in politics, responded to the times, and to his own emerging sense of identity, by expressing a wish to enlist in the Canadian army. He did not act on it immediately, but the idea was on his mind almost from the war's outset. For a professional hockey prospect, this was no small commit-ment. Even if one avoided being killed or maimed in action, the key years of development could be given over to training and fighting. One might well return too old, and too worn, to make it in the NHL.

Richard would, it turned out, have been safer in an army camp in England. During his first game with the Montreal

Canadiens of the Quebec Senior Hockey League—one rung below the "real" Habs—he crashed into the boards feet-first. As Howie Morenz had done four years earlier, he broke his left leg, although in just one spot, and wore a cast until Christmas. He didn't heal in time to resume the season, and instead worked his lathe at the CPR yards, bicycled and swam, played softball and boxed. He also tried, against his nature, not to brood. If he was now almost twenty, that meant Lucille was sixteen, still his girlfriend but also still too young for marriage. She lived with her parents in Bordeaux; he lived with his parents in the same neighbourhood. Teammates drank and smoked and chased girls, who liked hockey players. Richard drank beer after a game, but unlike his father—unlike most athletes, including the professionals who pitched brands in newspaper ads—he didn't smoke. Nor did he chase other girls; his cheerful, extroverted sweetheart was all he wanted. Their engagement, proper though it was, did not please her parents, even though he was earning forty dollars a week as a machinist, and a few more dollars playing hockey. The Norchets still thought them both too young.

Lucille was already helping him manage his dark moods and his disappointments, either by soothing words or the simple contrast of her personality. Halfway into his second season with the Senior Canadiens he got injured again, breaking a wrist. He returned for the playoffs and showed enough speed, tenacity, and skill to earn a tryout with the actual NHL squad in the fall. The Habs had a business reason for inviting Maurice Richard and another prospect named Marcel Bessette to try claiming a spot. The team, coached by Dick Irvin, of Hamilton, Ontario, and managed by NHL pioneer Tommy Gorman, a native of Ottawa, had only three French players on its roster. The apparently frail Richard, who brought fans to their feet with his headlong rushes, might also bring certain people, also named Bessette and Bouchard, Bilbeaut and Goupille, to the games. It helped that he was almost matinee-idol handsome, a happy subject for newspaper artists to sketch and easy on the eyes for any women who accompanied their dates to the Forum. And it didn't especially hurt that he spoke in reluctant monosyllables in French, and scarcely a word of English. Pre-television, and with print media willing to go along, Maurice Richard needed to be more a terror on ice, and presentable off it, than have any voice in any language.

Maurice and Lucille were finally married on September 12, 1942. He was twenty-one, she was seventeen, and the couple moved into a small apartment near Lafontaine Park— just as his parents had done. He still hadn't set foot inside the Forum; the first day of training camp was in three weeks, obliging him to ride the streetcar along St. Catherine Street into the west end. But he was an NHL prospect, and soon a signed rookie who, wearing number 15 and guaranteed a salary of $3,500 for the season, scored his first professional goal on November 8. Wasting no time, the *Montréal-Matin* reported: "The most spectacular goal of the evening, which brought back memories of the famous Howie Morenz, was scored by Maurice Richard, the popular left winger." Already, he was "popular," and resembled the late Morenz; already, he was being assigned a role—and not only to do with playing hockey.

On December 28, the bruising Boston defenceman Johnny Crawford levelled the Great French-Canadian Hope with a body check akin to an artillery shell going off nearby. Richard went down in agony, his leg again fractured, his rookie season in ruins. The five-foot-eleven, 190-pound Crawford made the All-Star team; Maurice Richard, five-ten and 180 pounds, his leg propped on a footstool, sat in the cramped living room of a small apartment listening to the games on the radio and stewing about whether, as many were now whispering, he was too fragile for the big leagues, especially given that the same limb, twice broken, might never heal properly. That, or he was just unlucky. All that skill and desire, along with an almost consuming need to score goals, couldn't offset a body that kept breaking. Management even initiated trade talks, hoping to unload their damaged goods. No one was interested.

It was in this mood of near despondency that Richard, who had spent his months of convalescence listening to Radio-Canada coverage of the war as well, resolved to enlist in the army for combat duty. The risks notwithstanding, he was far from the only player so inclined: nine members of the Detroit Red Wings and six Toronto Maple Leafs had recently joined up. Among his fellow Habs, only Winnipeg native Kenny Reardon volunteered to fight, and for a French Canadian, especially now that Mackenzie King had announced a referendum on conscription, a move met with loud, occasionally violent demonstrations around the city, the decision was fraught. In the summer he presented himself at a recruiting office for his physical. When X-rays revealed that neither his femur, ankle, nor even his wrist had healed properly from their hockey injuries, Richard was turned down for service. The ankle, in particular, was permanently misshapen, obliging him to adjust how he skated on it. But if being deemed physically unfit to assist in the military campaign newly underway in Sicily, or the pending invasion of Italy in September—the first sustained action for Canadian troops since the disaster at Dieppe—was a personal humiliation, it was also a prod to ready himself for the upcoming season. He trained hard for camp, and arrived healthy. His confidence that his ankle, wrist, or leg would hold, that he would not suffer another debilitating injury, was less assured. Doubts about his body's capacity to withstand the sport he played were now planted in his psyche. Like the deformed ankle and weak wrist, they were permanent as well—part of his character, and even of his dreams.

His second year started off slowly, and, sure enough, he dislocated a shoulder early on, missing several games. He also requested a sweater change, asking to wear number 9, in honour of the birth weight of his first child, Huguette. Richard waited at the hospital for hours while Lucille was in labour, jangly with nerves, and cried openly at the sight of his newborn. Neither the nervous waiting, nor the free tears, were how most men carried themselves in 1943. But Maurice Richard, it was already apparent, wasn't like most men: at once harder and more resolved, but also more sensitive and vulnerable—born, it seemed, without much emotional armour. The new father, and new number 9, was paired with high-scoring Elmer Lach and the veteran team captain, Hector "Toe" Blake. All three shot left-handed. In an inspired coaching decision, Dick Irvin switched Richard to right wing. His already patented move—swinging wide and bearing down on goal from a sharp angle, stymying defencemen, who had to either take the feet out from under him or jump on him, and unnerving goalies, especially with his head up, his dark gaze alarming—was much harder to stop with his good arm, and his naturally stronger leg, keeping defenders at bay.

Starting early in 1944, Richard scored thirty goals in the final thirty games, and teammates, fatigued from chasing him in practice and noticing his ability to accelerate with the force of a sprung weapon, started calling him "the Rocket." They did so in English, the only language most of them spoke and the lingua franca of the coach and management. Richard, seated in the dressing room next to Emile "Butch" Bouchard, a stalwart defenceman with good English, must have listened while the nickname was translated for him. *Tu patines comme une fusée,* Bouchard told him. *You skate like a rocket.* He had already been called "the Comet" and, less poetically, "Bones," on account of his frailty, and was soon the embodiment of the "Flying Frenchmen," a term describing the swift, fluid style of Montreal Canadiens teams over the next four decades. "The Comet," *la comète;* "Bones," *des os;* "the Flying Frenchmen," *les Flying Frenchmen*—like "the Rocket," *le Rocket,* English words for French phenomena.

The nickname suited his style, and the times. The twenty-two-year-old did skate and play like the human equivalent of a missile. Across the Atlantic, German V1 and V2 rockets were done pummelling England. Shortly, the Allies, breaching "fortress Europe" in Normandy, would return the awesome firepower upon German cities. Thrust, drive, power: the attributes of an army on the march and a winger striding up the ice were being paralleled; the drive of a righteous force, the Allied armies upon Berlin, was shortly to be conflated with an athlete's determined march on scoring records and championships, also for a just cause. In the off-season, and in the wake of D-Day, Elmer Lach took up a job at an airplane factory and Toe Blake in a shipyard. Maurice Richard operated a lathe in a munitions factory. That same summer, with much of Europe engulfed in ferocious, desperate warfare, he would try to enlist again, offering his services as a machinist. Lacking a high-school degree and having not yet completed his technical trade certificate, he was once more refused. He vowed to finish his training while playing for the Canadiens that winter.

The Maurice Richard who was turned down again by the army in 1944 was a member of the newly crowned Stanley Cup champions. The Canadiens had won their first Cup since 1930 in April, and after scoring all five goals in a playoff game, for which he was named the first, second, and third stars, he was also dubbed "V5." Being "the Rocket" on the NHL's top squad did not preclude him from either working in a factory off-season, or from wishing to enlist in the military at the lowest rank—a private. His salary with the Habs was more than he could earn as a machinist, but not enough to buy a house, or take summers off. He earned as much as a schoolteacher but not as much as a bank executive; he still rode the streetcar and paid monthly rent. As was the custom before athletes' salaries soared, friends and team boosters organized a tribute to him, an opportunity to express gratitude for his play and to compensate for his modest income. Twelve hundred people attended, including retired greats Aurèle Joliat and Leo Dandurand, along with his parents, Onésime and Alice. Gifts included a wallet, a cigarette lighter, a coffee table, and a set of luggage. He took his regular shift at the munitions plant the next morning.

THAT AUTUMN, six thousand spectators showed up for a pre-season scrimmage at the Forum. Toe Blake and Elmer Lach were league stars, and management had brought up a brilliant new goaltender the previous season named Bill Durnan. But the autograph hunters, the clusters of kids waiting by the dressing room door, were most anxious to meet Maurice "Rocket" Richard. This was something new for him, and for the recently struggling franchise, which was suddenly *Nos Glorieux* among Quebecers—"our glorious ones," emblems of French-Canadian pride and achievement. Both rose, in a sense, to the sudden occasion. Teams played fifty games a season then, and the Habs lost just eight of those in 1944–45. Richard, competing with teammate Lach for the scoring title, was soon on pace to score a remarkable one goal per game. No player had ever scored more than forty-four, and though there was talk of the record being tarnished by the diminished skill level in a war-depleted league, on the night he scored his forty-third goal in a sold-out Forum—his pursuit of "fifty in fifty" was filling seats and newspapers alike—he received a two-minute ovation. When he tied the record in Toronto against the Maple Leafs, now the Habs' fiercest rivals, the hostile crowd barely acknowledged the feat. Not until the final period of the season's final game, playing the Bruins in Boston, did he set the record.

To score fifty goals in as many games, he'd had to display superb stickhandling, a quick wrist shot, and a low, accurate backhand, as well as an ability to blow past defenders with abrupt surges and relentless end-to-end rushes. Two incidents from the season quickly entered Rocket lore. In December, with Lucille pregnant again, he moved his family to a larger apartment in the same neighbourhood. Though his brother-in-law helped out, Richard ended up lugging tables, beds, and sofas up an outdoor staircase to the second-floor flat. He did so on a frigid winter day, and in a snowstorm. He had a game that same night, and ruefully informed his coach he doubted he would be effective. (His brother-in-law bet he wouldn't manage a point.) Richard scored five goals and earned three assists in a blowout. Two months later he famously scored with a 210-pound defence-man named Earl Seibert hanging off his shoulders. The referee of that game in Boston gave an account: "Earl Seibert jumped on his back. Jumped on his back! Put his arms around him. And his legs around him. The Rocket never broke stride. He went in, deked the goaltender, scored a goal, and shook Seibert and threw him in the corner."

Earl Seibert's failed takedown foreshadowed the circumstances Richard would face each game. Starting that second season, he had to get used to opposing teams doing everything they could to intimidate, frustrate, and provoke him. Early in the campaign, coaches began assigning a player, sometimes two, to shadow the twenty-four-year-old around the ice, and to hook, hold, slash, and even spear the speed and spirit out of him. Either he absorbed the punishment, as he did with Seibert, or he returned it in kind. A highly strung athlete, Richard proved easy to wind up, either through violent, illegal play or verbal taunts, and he had no capacity to abide uncalled penalties or unanswered insults. He was known from early on to be both physically frail and volatile, and the best place for the Rocket, from the opposition's perspective, was either in the dressing room, getting a swollen ankle iced, or in the penalty box, stewing for five minutes for a fight he hadn't instigated but hadn't backed down from either.

Coaches sent out their toughest guys to enrage him. NHL players did their own fighting then; there were no enforcers or protectors, no one to shield a star athlete from the purposeful aggressions of a thug. The New York Rangers kept a player named Bob Dill, a marginal talent with a background as an amateur boxer. He went after Richard twice on the same night at Madison Square Garden, once on the ice and the second time in the penalty box, which teams shared. The first fight, Richard knocked Dill unconscious with a single left jab; the second time, he did the same. In the game against the Maple Leafs in which he broke the record for most goals in a season, no fewer than six fights broke out, including a bench-clearing brawl and an altercation between players and fans. "This Richard is a great player," a former NHL star commented that night. "He's fast, game, and powerful. Really strong. Look at the way he fights off checks, tears loose from them, fights for the puck."

Major Conn Smythe, owner of the Toronto Maple Leafs and newly returned from the war, watched his performance in that game. The next day he called the Canadiens' general manager and offered $25,000 cash for Richard's contract. That was a considerable sum, the equivalent of five or six player salaries, and for Smythe, who thought poorly of most non-WASPs in general, and of French Canadians in particular, a concession to Richard's evident courage and charisma. In the eyes of the bigoted Smythe, he was a rarity: a fighting Frenchman, as much guts as finesse, grit as grace.

The Canadiens turned him down. Maurice Richard wasn't only nearing the fabled fifty-goals-in-as-many-games mark; he was the reason ticket agents at the Forum were disappointing several thousand would-be spectators each night. He was the fresh face of the franchise, and perfect for the times: French-speaking, attractive, and fiery, wild in the rink and reserved and polite away from it. With the fall of Berlin and the suicide of Adolf Hitler in April 1945, World War II was near done, a victory that even the most ambivalent French Canadian could celebrate. Since the previous August, too, the oligarch Maurice Duplessis was back in office as premier, despite having received fewer votes than Adélard

Godbout. The electoral map favoured rural Quebec, where people were far more in the thrall of Duplessis's inward vision of the province, and had voted the reformer Liberal out, despite his dominant showing among working-class French in Montreal. Even Camillien Houde, the impish mayor recently released from internment, was about to resume his old job at city hall. Godbout's good, secular governance, a precursor of the Quiet Revolution, was soon swept into obscurity by the re-ascendancy of demagogic politics and deeply conservative, Church-backed, Anglo and French money-fuelled rule. Those French Canadians, once more designated as "small," would soon need a hero to avenge all the wrongs being done to them, by whomever was presented as the wrongdoers; someone who could embody a feeling of, if not empowerment, then righteous fury and power, boosting their self-esteem with his stick and living out their revenge fantasies through his fists. Conn Smythe never had a chance of poaching Maurice Richard. The Montreal Canadiens, and the hidden powers in Quebec, had built themselves a Rocket, one designed to hold back, not launch, social change. And they were going to set it off.

CHAPTER FOUR

La Noirceur

I kiss his [the priest's] ring, and he kisses my a**.
MAURICE DUPLESSIS

The Montreal Forum that Maurice Richard first stepped inside in 1943 was drab and dilapidated. Of the nine thousand seats, half were benches far above the surface, sold for sixty-five cents each on game day. Mockingly dubbed "The Millionaires," the rabble higher up were separated from the better-paying patrons below by fencing that resembled chicken wire. Though the divide between those on benches and those with seats was often presented as linguistic—French above, English below—it was actually a reflection of the city's class distinctions. The working-class French who suffered splinters and viewed the action through fencing were mixed in with their Irish and Scots brethren from Pointe-Saint-Charles and Verdun. The English-speaking elite, leaders of the city's still fabulously wealthy business community, held season tickets in the proper seats nearer the ice alongside the

francophone bourgeoisie of Outremont and the more affluent Jews of Westmount. The Canadiens organization didn't
practise seating segregation—in theory, anyone could purchase a ticket anywhere in the Forum—but arrangements
played out along class lines that were only secondarily language divides. It was also true that among the taunts Maurice
Richard endured whenever he played in any other of the
cities in the NHL—Toronto, Chicago, Detroit, New York,
and Boston—the epithets related to his so-called "race," such
as "Frog" or "Pea Souper," would occasionally include a
request that he "speak white." (It didn't matter if the oppo-
nent was a team based in the United States: three-quarters of
the players in the league were English Canadians, and knew
where to cut with their verbal knives.) The notion of English
Montrealers, or even English Canadians, being "white" and
the French majority inside Quebec, and minority outside it,
being non-white or ethnic, was ridiculous, but the metaphor
spoke to the lingering ugliness of the early century's obsession
with race and racial difference.

In 1946 the new team manager, Frank Selke, repainted
the seats into red, white, and blue sections, each priced
accordingly. If the arrangement didn't much alter the
reality that the affluent wound up closer to the ice and
the marginal farther away, it did at least eliminate the wire

barriers, with their heavy symbolic suggestion. Had a particular athlete from another team in Montreal decided to
attend a hockey game in the fall, he would certainly have
registered the psychic weight of chicken-wire fencing.
Twenty-seven-year-old baseball player Jackie Robinson, then
an outfielder for the Montreal Royals of the Class AAA
International League, brought home a championship that
season through his powerful batting and flawless fielding. In
appreciation, fans hoisted Robinson on their shoulders and
paraded him around Delorimier Downs in Montreal East,
where the Royals played. The following year Robinson, having been embraced by Montreal during his brief stay there—
everywhere in the States he travelled, in contrast, he was
taunted, the epithets brutally racial, all related to his skin
colour—was called up by the Brooklyn Dodgers, becoming
the first African-American allowed into the National
League.

In the renovated Forum, now able to accommodate
twelve thousand, the wiring behind the goals was replaced
with glass. Patrons still rested their elbows on the boards
along either side, ducking pucks, sticks and, occasionally,
bodies propelled over the top. From rinkside, red ticket
holders, dressed in suits, ties, and overcoats, with the women
in dresses and hats—a Habs game was a big night out

among the more moneyed, a see-and-be-seen event—could observe the expressions on players' faces and overhear their exchanges, including those taunts. Suits and dresses were also occasionally sprayed with gladiator spit and sweat during the exhilarating fist fights. (The athletes, in turn, skated through a pall of cigarette smoke hanging over the surface.) In 1946, *Hockey Night in Canada* was still only a radio event; the first television broadcast was six years away. The games remained intimate and visceral, especially in the era before wraparound glass created distance between spectator and athlete and helmets and masks began to hide the players' emotions. Even the policy of a shared penalty box, which meant opponents could resume their fight inside the cubicle, contributed. Before and after games, too, players were accessible. Fans could approach these rugged young men as they exited the arena in their suits and ties, or while they waited on the platform at Windsor Station to board overnight trains to Boston and New York.

Maurice Richard, also immaculately groomed—under Lucille's tutelage, he favoured tailored dark suits and visited his barber late in the afternoon on game days, where his shave and trim attracted kids at the shop window—wore his feelings on his face no less than he wore the team logo on his chest. He could communicate only minimal remarks to his English linemates, and rarely smiled, but his body language did some of the talking: circling in frustration during interruptions in play, lowering his head and banging his stick on the ice in disappointment at a poor shift. His fearsome dark eyes were most eloquent, registering desire, determination, and, more often than not, anger. Pretty much everyone in the building could "read" Maurice Richard. Teammates knew when he was ready to explode and opposition players sensed when their grabbing, poking, and needling was getting to him. Referees too surmised when he was reaching the boiling point. Fans could also tell when the Rocket was about to go off. His ability to raise the temperature inside the Forum on the coldest winter nights made for electrifying sporting experiences. This was especially true once the expression of his gift and indomitable will came to be viewed as a simulacrum of a people's own impatience and potential. Of their very souls, even.

Before television, these nightly dramas could only be captured visually through grainy still photographs and artists' sketches. But words were readily available to render his exploits immortal. They flowed from fans leaving the Forum exchanging accounts of a spectacular goal, or the CBC radio announcer or, better still, Michel Normandin, the hypereloquent, florid Radio-Canada play-by-play host, filling the eyes of listeners gathered around their radios in Bordeaux and Laval, Lac St-Jean and Rivière-du-Loup, with vivid, unforgettable "pictures" of the Rocket in action. Whatever the source, starting in the mid-1940s the on-ice marvels of Maurice Richard began entering into cultural lore. Sports legends—of scoring five goals after moving house, of carrying a defenceman on his back like a sack of grain—were thus born by the oldest method known: oral storytelling, the tales growing taller and taller with every telling.

THE LATE 1940S SAW THE CANADIENS WIN one more Cup, in 1946, and then struggle to match the firepower of first the Toronto Maple Leafs and then the Detroit Red Wings. As had been predicted, the league changed complexion once the already tough men returned from the war that much more toughened. Along with the surging talent level in the NHL came the enshrinement of gladiatorial hockey. First the Leafs under the martial Smythe, and then the Red Wings steered by "Terrible" Ted Lindsay and the young Gordie Howe, played hard each night. They also played rough and, like armies at war, employed an arsenal of tactics to intimidate, humiliate, and finally defeat the enemy. No quarter was given; each of the now sixty regular-season games was a battle of skills played out under the constant threat of physical assault and psychological battery. To some, this brand of hockey—nurtured on the prairies and in small-town Ontario, its proponents mostly farm boys and the sons of mill workers and miners, brawny and raw-boned, disavowing flash or flair, respectful young men off the ice but foul-mouthed, stick-wielding terrors on it—stood in stark contrast to how the sport was played in Quebec. There, the "Flying Frenchmen" inspired pride with their swift skating and skilled puck-handling, their end-to-end dashes that brought fans to their feet. The contrast reflected the differences between the two Canadas, the two cultures, even the two languages. Inside Quebec, how Gordie Howe or Ted Lindsay played hockey, or more exactly how they played hockey against *our* boys, also the sons of miners and mill workers, spoke to the divide between that "other Canada," a continent-wide land mass comprising, apparently, thousands of miles of wheat fields and another thousand of mountains, and the Saint Lawrence River valley and Saguenay, the Beauce and the Gaspé.

Only some of these perceptions were accurate. The Habs themselves were still a majority English squad, and even a few years into the future, with the pieces of the dynastic team in place, would continue to feature key players with names like Harvey and Moore. Nor were the contrasts in

"English" and "French" playing styles that vast, or the allegiances of fans in English Canada, especially in the West, by any means certain to automatically support the Toronto Maple Leafs. But among French Canadians it was coming to be held as axiomatic that the National Hockey League—with its 75 percent English players and 100 percent English owners, its mostly English referees, its head offices in the Sun Life building on Dominion Square in downtown Montreal (then the largest edifice in the British Empire), and its unilingual new president, the lawyer, Rhodes Scholar, and decorated war veteran Clarence Campbell—now also had a sanctioned English-Canadian style of play, one designed to stymie, bruise, and generally grind down French athletes, show them their proper, and lowly, place in the scheme of things.

Maurice Richard, the exemplar of French-Canadian hockey, also appeared to suffer accordingly in the postwar era. His goal total dropped from fifty in 1944–45 to twenty-seven the following season, and though he rebounded to score forty-five times in the 1946–47 campaign, the Habs lost the championship to their much-hated rivals, the Toronto Maple Leafs. Worse, the team, already dealing with the absence of its other leading scorer, Elmer Lach, out due to a vicious hit that resulted in a skull fracture, had to play without Richard for a key game in the finals. He was suspended by Clarence Campbell for having drawn blood, twice, the previous night, first cutting one Maple Leaf player above the eye with his stick and then cracking another over the head, ripping open his scalp. Both actions, done out of retaliation, showed just how violent his temper could be, and how extreme his responses. Fuming, he sat listening to the third game in his hotel room in Toronto, tossing the radio out the window in disgust at the outcome. His cool went missing, and with it the Stanley Cup; lost, it seemed to many in Quebec, to a near conspiracy of an Anglo president, biased referees, and the hostile fans in Maple Leaf Gardens in Toronto, a city of bigots, their distemper likely exacerbated by absurd liquor laws that kept entire neighbourhoods dry.

In the French media, few examined how reckless Richard's own actions had been during that playoff series, or how consequential to his team. They liked, and recognized, his passion and emotional intensity. They liked him. The wrongs being done were to Maurice Richard, to the Montreal Canadiens, to French Canadians, in equal measure; the linkage was that direct and totalizing, and the only vindication for the "small people" was for Richard to score all the time and the Canadiens to win the Stanley Cup every spring. Nothing else would do, and the reality that one player, no matter how gifted or tenacious, couldn't manage a goal a game and that one team, no matter how good, couldn't win every season, was immaterial.

The Habs' defeat by the Maple Leafs in April 1947 augured ill. They would not claim another championship for seven years. Darkness, *la noirceur,* engulfed the team.

NOW IN HIS LATE TWENTIES, with a wife and three small children to support, the naturally diffident Maurice Richard went looking for an increase in his salary the following September. He was the most famous athlete in Quebec, recognized around Montreal and across the province thanks to newspaper photos and sketches and his first product endorsements, and he wanted to buy a house in the city's north end, near his aging parents. The pay raise was not an unreasonable request; he had been recently awarded the Hart Trophy as the league's most valuable player for the 1946–47 season, and had been filling the Forum each night and boosting attendances in every other city around the league since the war. People paid to see him play, mostly for his explosive talent but also for the elaborate taunt-and-bait that accompanied his every shift. But when his awkward meeting with Frank Selke went nowhere—Selke insisted he complete his current contract—he and defenceman Emile

Bouchard held out during training camp, their own tiny work stoppage. Arguably, here was the heart and soul of the team, offence and defence respectively, the two most physically courageous athletes, never quitting, never backing down. Here as well were two "Flying Frenchmen" who refuted the popular (if incorrect) contention elsewhere in Canada that hockey in Quebec was played by soft, highly strung sorts. Bouchard was team captain, and Richard one of his alternates.

But Selke still refused. He had every reason to hold tough with his stars. Management was well aware that they "owned" these athletes, and could count, as all league owners did, on them feeling privileged to play for one of the six big teams. With the majority of players coming from working-class backgrounds, managers like Selke or, more notoriously, Red Wings' boss Jack Adams, took it for granted that these young men would measure their salaries not as commensurate with the income they generated for the franchises but as superior to what they might earn working in a mill or driving a truck. And so, on the day of the first game of the season, Richard and Bouchard, humiliated by their overseers, abandoned their requests to be fairly paid. (Rumours circulated that Selke actually imposed a pay cut on the league's MVP, as punishment.) A nagging knee injury ended up shortening Richard's season, and Montreal didn't even make the playoffs. Next season, the 1948–49 campaign, they did, but were eliminated quickly, and the great Rocket managed just twenty goals. Once again, he fought injuries, other players, referees, Clarence Campbell; in one game he left the penalty box to argue a call and the referee, fearing for his own safety, summoned the police to have the NHL's biggest draw escorted from the ice. And, once again, he came up short.

Expectations, both his own and those of others, were weighing on him. Insouciance, the ability to make the difficult look easy, to play a sport at the highest level with the apparent joy of a kid playing shinny on a frozen river: none of these qualities, evident in certain great athletes, were part of Maurice Richard's makeup. Hockey for him was all or nothing, each and every night. You score and win, or you don't score and you lose. Win, and you've done your job, acquitted yourself as an athlete, a man, a French Canadian. Lose, and you've failed, disappointed, in all three categories. Nothing could look easy because nothing was; few smiles broke out, few moments of levity emerged; this was a grave, serious business. A serious business and a solitary one, with no individual in the stands, in the press box, even alongside him on the bench, really able to feel the responsibility as he did, to share the burden he had either been given, or taken on—or both. Hardly a surprise that the strain showed on his face and in his body language. Hardly a surprise, either, that it manifested itself in his righteous retaliations, his occasional losses of composure.

Being Maurice Richard, there was no avoiding the hacks and trips, the slashing and spearing, being blindsided by a check and run into the boards face, or feet, first. There was no avoiding either the duels of words, fists, and sticks. Cuts, stitches, bruises, swollen joints, sprains—the proverbial getting "banged up" over the course of a long season—went scarcely more noticed by him than did mosquito bites. But skull and bone fractures, torn ligaments, and ruptured discs? These kinds of injuries—season-ending, even livelihood-threatening—were beginning to keep him awake with anxiety.

The NHL career of his "Punch Line" mate, Toe Blake, had ended in 1948 with a fractured ankle. Blake, at least, was thirty-six, his playing days already on the wane. But two years later stalwart defenceman Ken Reardon, just twenty-nine—Richard's own age—also retired, citing shoulders ruined by too many collisions with players, goalposts, boards. And neither Blake nor Reardon, nor Elmer Lach or Emile Bouchard, were targets as big as Maurice Richard. He was the franchise player, the hope. He was the new Howie

Morenz. Morenz, who died at just thirty-four. Had he perished in the war? No, he was killed playing hockey for the Canadiens.

"My stomach nerves were very bad for a while," Richard would later admit. "I don't sleep, maybe four or five hours a night. The rest of the time I lie awake."

Maurice Richard wasn't only inarticulate and inward. He was earnest and deeply anxious, ill suited, on one level, to the growing pressures and expectations he was facing as a professional athlete and a high-profile member of a restless majority. At the same time, it was his intensity, even his anxiety—to perform well, to remain deserving of those accolades and, soon, idolatries—along with phenomenal reserves of physical skill and courage, that made him the *only* man likely to withstand the pressures and live up to the expectations. Similarly, his stay-at-home nature, an instinctive sense that he could only truly be himself in Montreal, ensured that he would never retreat, never hide, and certainly never flee. People knew where to find him, either at the Forum or in the city; people knew who he was. He was the Montreal-born child of Gaspé émigrés and the machinist-trained son of an Angus Yards worker. He was the blue-collar Bordeaux boy with the Bordeaux wife, herself the daughter of a butcher, who were now raising their growing family in neighbouring Ahuntsic.

Maurice Richard, in short, wasn't going anywhere.

Regardless, Conn Smythe tried buying him again for the Maple Leafs in 1949, and again in 1951. Both times the Habs declined the ever-larger sums; to have sold Maurice Richard now would have been like retailing the working-class French-Canadian identity, stripped down for parts. By the late 1940s he was being dubbed "Saint Maurice," and though he made the sign of the cross before he stepped onto the ice before each period—*au nom du Père et du Fils et du Saint-Esprit, Amen*—it was French Canadians who were praying to him.

Lucille did what she could to share his burden. Even without the 1947 raise, the Richards had gone ahead and bought a two-story house in the village of Ahuntsic-Cartierville, about a half-mile from the waterfront of Rivière-des-Prairies, where Maurice had skated as a boy. He lived the same distance from his parents and still occasionally went there for Sunday dinner, taking his children along and exchanging a few words—all he could muster with most people, including siblings—with his fourteen-year-old brother, Henri, himself a junior hockey sensation. (Two other brothers, Jacques and Claude, were also prospects.) On game days Lucille drove with him to the Forum, usually in companionable silence, and sat in the red section with the

other players' wives, where, like her husband, she was learning English, courtesy of deepening friendships with English-
speaking colleagues. Then she waited while he showered and
signed autographs to ride back with him to the north end
afterwards. There, he might talk a little about the game, how
he had played, what he could have done better. If stuck in
traffic, or waiting at a light, he might hear directly the opin-
ions of Montrealers walking home from the Forum, or those
who'd listened to Michel Normandin's account of the game
on Radio-Canada. They would call out, ask him to roll
down his window so they could be clearly heard. He usually
stopped; he usually listened. Likewise, if the Richards went
to a restaurant, always a family dining establishment, he
would attend patiently to everyone who approached their
table, standing for the women, shaking hands with the men,
signing autographs, wincing his shy, sincere smile. The fancy
restaurants patronized by red season ticket holders did not
suit him at all; his only appearances in such places were
when management threw the players a party, usually after a
championship, at the Queen Elizabeth Hotel or in a private
club.

Richard's failed 1947 campaign to gain a salary increase
echoed larger patterns at play in the Quebec of Maurice
Duplessis. In February 1949 asbestos workers, poorly paid

and suffering dangerous conditions, walked off their jobs at four mines around the province. For six weeks the strikers held out. Duplessis, viewing the action as evidence of creeping socialism, backed the owners, sending in squads of police to protect the mines and later encouraging the hiring of scabs and the use of brutality to end the walkout. The Catholic Church, normally his staunch ally in maintaining the status quo, split on the asbestos strike, with a key figure, the archbishop of Montreal, Joseph Carbonneau, encouraging the faithful to donate to the strikers and their families. The strike ended badly in the short term—a minimal pay hike, jobs lost, men blacklisted for life—but augured real change. One young intellectual who had worked with the strikers, Pierre Elliott Trudeau, portrayed the labour action as "a violent announcement that a new era had begun." He and some friends went to work agitating for a new Quebec in the pages of the journal *Cité Libre*.

Behind the asbestos strike loomed a larger conflict. The now-suppressed secular values of Adélard Godbout's Quebec—itself a manifestation of the liberalism of everyone from Prime Minister Louis St. Laurent to the then secretary of the Catholic Workers Confederation of Canada, Jean Marchard, along with that of younger intellectuals like Pierre Trudeau and Gérard Pelletier—were at odds with

Maurice Duplessis's heavy-handed governance of the province. In 1950, however, the emerging thoughts of Trudeau or journalist René Lévesque about social change were yet a small noise, and one unheard by the vast majority of French Canadians still living in the shade, if not outright darkness, of the Union Nationale era. In the name of the small people he claimed to champion, Duplessis suppressed civil liberties and starved social services, kept the education system backward and stamped out workers' rights. He made a mockery of elections by the frank, cynical employment of patronage and coercion. He did kiss the rings of priests and, more often than not, the Church returned the favour, grateful to have its vision of the province's Catholic flock—rural or small town, unilingual, busy having babies and playing hockey—held up as the "real" Quebec by *le chef* himself.

In 1951, the Canadiens feted Maurice Richard before a game against the Red Wings. Regular tributes, off-season banquets with "gifts" from fans, continued to substitute for proper salary increases, ensuring that men like him would indeed claim it a privilege just to play for the *bleu, blanc, rouge.* When Richard was given a new car by his admirers, he made a brief, awkward speech to the crowd in French. He also shook the hand of his nemesis, Gordie Howe, with whom he could now at least converse in his improved English. In the stands that night were the three dominant politicians of the time in Montreal: Prime Minister St. Laurent, Premier Duplessis, and Mayor Houde. Each was keen to claim Richard as his own. If any should have won his support, it might have been St. Laurent and the Liberal Party, federal and provincial, for whom those Montrealers who filled the Forum, whether francophone or anglophone, working class or elite, tended to vote. Instead, believing the narrative that the Union Nationale stood up for French Canadians and kept the province strong inside Canada, the Rocket ended up campaigning for Duplessis in the 1952 general election. The other famous Maurice, as the media dubbed him, helped get the politician and his party re-elected, albeit with a smaller majority than they had in 1948. Duplessis, in turn, never passed up a chance to get his photo taken with Maurice Richard. Why would he? Rocket Richard, *le chef,* the two Maurices, both Catholics, both proud Quebecers, both fighters, tenacious and unstoppable, for their people.

If Quebec languished in historic and political gloom during these years, so did Maurice Richard. He was a warrior, but one fighting in darkness, certain there was a battle yet unable to truly see the field or distinguish enemies from allies. Of what exactly was he even a symbol? Of quiet defiance and steady resistance, of an incremental awakening of an entire people? Or, less happily, of the ultimate "small" French Canadian being played for a sucker by church and state, the accidental company man shilling for interests that weren't really his own and that didn't deserve the imprimatur of his dignity and ferocity?

Even with fellow players, and their collective interests, he could not quite tell friend from foe. In the early 1950s, Red Wings star Ted Lindsay began agitating for player pensions and greater access to information about how team revenue was distributed. The league was regressive, the owners powerful and shameless, in frank, almost mocking, collusion to keep the athletes underpaid and disunified. Lindsay's heroic efforts weren't squashed by the NHL for a few years, but from the start he found no ally in the game's biggest attraction. "Terrible" Ted Lindsay was a skilled player who was also a notorious scrapper, all elbows and knees and fingers to the eyes, and he was one of the few who had fought the Rocket and not badly lost (most viewed the 1944 brawl as a bloody tie). Lindsay had been a constant on-ice nag ever since, spearing, hooking, and taunting him every game, and lately he had often been the victor, with the Red Wings winning the Stanley Cup in 1950 and again in 1952. Richard could not even bring himself to mutter Ted Lindsay's name aloud, let alone view him as an ally.

Nor, for that matter, could he envision confronting management. He was too reticent to be a good spokesman for his rights, rather than his obligations, as a professional hockey player. So much so that when the Canadiens decided to send someone to lure the young centre Jean Béliveau, then happily ensconced as a member of the Quebec Aces in the senior league, they bypassed Richard in favour of Emile Bouchard. The well-spoken Bouchard could "sell" the Habs to Béliveau, emphasizing the glory of the franchise and the need for French Canadians to stick together in support of their kind of hockey. While a decent, agreeable person, Richard couldn't be counted on to successfully express those values or even make a compelling case for the twenty-two-year-old to join the team. (When Béliveau finally showed at training camp, he brought along a lawyer and a financial adviser to his meeting with Selke, negotiating the biggest contract in league history.) The Rocket *was* those values and *was* that tradition, but he was also alone and apart.

A photo from *La grande noirceur* captured his singular status. On April 8, 1952, in a playoff game at the Forum against the Boston Bruins, Richard barrelled down the ice with his head unwisely down. Leo Labine, a fearsome winger, checked him hard, sending him face-first into the knee of another Boston player. Knocked out cold, he lay flat on the surface, a deep cut opened above his left eye. Revived by smelling salts—the team doctor knew he would despise being carried off on a stretcher—a wobbly Richard was helped to the dressing room and stitched up. Though unable to recall what had happened or what the score was, he returned to the bench with four minutes left in a tied game. Coach Irvin, aware he might have a concussion, still put him on, and he responded by taking a pass at centre ice, cutting in from the right and angling hard across the front of the net—his classic move, making him unstoppable because of his strength, low centre of gravity, and ability to protect his stick with his left hand. He scored; the Forum erupted; the Habs won the series.

The photo showed Boston goalie Jim "Sugar" Henry, his own right eye blackened, shaking hands with a clearly dazed Maurice Richard, blood streaming from the bandaged cut. Though other players are visible in the background, fringed in black, they are unimportant: in the cropped version of the image that soon became iconic, the two figures at the front are all that matter. Richard is upright, meeting the goaltender's gaze despite his evident discomfort. Henry returns the eye contact while literally bowing before him, his expression one of humility and respect. The image belongs to a nineteenth-century painting of a Napoleonic battlefield, two commanders, one vanquished and the other victorious, both raw from battle, the victor grave and dignified while his enemy accords him due respect.

In the dressing room, Richard wept with exhaustion and emotion. "Everything went black," he told reporters of the hit. "I didn't know where I was."

CHAPTER FIVE

A Riot Going On

Richard, my brother, has been killed.
ANDRÉ LAURENDEAU, TITLE OF OPINION PIECE
IN *LE DEVOIR*, MARCH 21, 1955

It was a long time coming, and probably unavoidable. Imperious, icy Clarence Campbell and the American-dominated, English-speaking NHL versus kingly, hot-blooded Maurice Richard and the awakening aspirations of his French subjects. In the spring of 1953, with the Canadiens finally winning another Stanley Cup, Richard escalated his war with the league. The hostilities, simmering since Campbell took over as president in 1946, had followed a familiar pattern. The Rocket, hauled down with impunity or slashed across the ankle without any whistle blown, called a "French pea soup" and "dirty French bastard" by players and coaches, would explode, using fists and stick as summary revenge. He would end up in the penalty box, or be ejected, and then fined and sometimes suspended by the league head office, under the presidency of *le patron*.

A typical incident in New York was recorded by the newest innovation: television cameras, which began showing NHL games during the '52–53 season. Unsure how to film a sport with swift-moving action and a careening black rubber disc, the primitive equipment's limitations exacerbated by inadequate lighting in the arenas, TV tended at first to offer narrated highlights of games. A Canadiens–Rangers match from that season, filmed by the Madison Square Garden crew, caught the Rocket in ferocious mid-career form, prowling the ice between whistles with his stick held high, daring anyone to sneak-attack him. When a fight breaks out in front of the Habs goal, the voice-over tells viewers to "watch the right side of the screen as the climax comes as Maurice Richard cuts a two-inch gash in Eddie Culman's scalp. Eddie's all right," the voice adds of the grainy footage of Richard expertly clipping the side of the Ranger player's head with the tip of his stick, "but he needed eight stitches." The three-minute film ended with a declaration that was shortly to become the standard summation—half appreciation, half head-shaking dismay—of the feral Canadian sport: "Another hockey donnybrook."

In an earlier outburst, Richard, believing he had been

unfairly penalized for a play in which *he* was driven headfirst
into a goalpost, coming up once more bloody, was ejected for
pounding a Detroit player inside the penalty box. Furious at
being sent off, he fumed all night in his hotel room. The next
morning in the hotel lobby he spotted the referee who had
officiated the game and grabbed the man by the collar, cursing him. He did so in his heavily accented English and in
front of strangers, and likely struck onlookers as an unhinged
foreigner. Clarence Campbell, noting that the women of
Detroit had been within earshot of his tirade, declared such
behaviour unacceptable. But instead of a suspension, the
league fined Richard a hundred dollars. Not long after, the
notoriously inarticulate athlete tried using the media to air
his grievances. The Montreal paper *Samedi-Dimanche* had
been publishing a column "by" Maurice Richard for years,
calling him up once a week and extracting sufficient detail
about life as a sports icon to allow a staff writer to piece
together seven hundred words. Until recently, the column
had been bland stuff, of interest only to diehard fans.
Published in French, it was also of little wider import to the
NHL—although Campbell's office monitored it.

Starting early in 1954, the league had good reason to
track *"Le tour du chapeau"* ("Hat Trick"), as the column was
titled. Richard began using the space to speak his mind, to

strike out at enemies and, intentionally or not, widen the struggle between himself and the NHL until it could be easily cast in the largest political terms possible. One week he accused Campbell of imposing especially harsh fines and suspensions on French-Canadian members of the Habs. Another column questioned whether English players were being given "paper assists" to ensure they won the scoring title. Richard also declared that the president, who attended most games at the Forum, his white hair and officer bearing putting him in good company with the CEOs and executives near the ice, routinely cheered for the opposition. "What did Campbell do?" Maurice Richard asked in *Samedi-Dimanche,* "when Jean Béliveau was deliberately injured twice by Bill Mosienko of Chicago and Jack Evans of the Rangers? No penalty, no fine, no suspension. Did he suspend Gordie Howe of Detroit when he almost knocked out Dollard St. Laurent's eye? No!

"Strange," the Rocket concluded, "that only Dick Irvin and I have the courage to risk our livelihood by defending our rights against such a dictator."

Calling Campbell a dictator proved too much. The league president chewed out Canadiens' manager Frank Selke, who, in turn, demanded that Richard issue an apology—or else. Maurice Richard, now the NHL's all-time leading scorer, backed down, withdrawing the remarks and apologizing "humbly and sincerely." He also agreed to drop the newspaper column, which meant a loss of income, and to post a thousand-dollar "good faith" bond with the league, as assurance against any future fines that might be levied against him. It was a rout by Campbell, a public humiliation of a very proud athlete. Richard, believing as always that he was helpless before the owners, understood it as such, as did French Quebec. Deep insult was taken by all. The thousand dollars he had to post with the league office was put up by a group of fans who had been paying his fines for years. Just as team boosters, mostly French Canadian, supplied Richard and other stars with gifts, the paying of the bond by private citizens was an investment, in effect, in the Rocket's rebelliousness and, more and more, his insurrection. Bypassing the middleman in these exchanges—i.e., the Canadiens organization, which represented English-speaking, Anglo Montreal—marked its own kind of rebellion, a tribal gesture.

The 1953 championship notwithstanding, the thirty-three-year-old Richard was convinced he was being victimized because of widespread hostility toward his kind. He felt the French minority position in Canada, and North America, in his bones, their status as a vulnerable, misunderstood group at sea in a continent of English speech and

Anglo-Saxon manners. He was also beginning to sense that he was implicated in a larger fight for justice. The battle was clearly not on the scale of Jackie Robinson's struggle with institutional racism in baseball. Nor was it entirely a French–English divide. Loyal teammates Dickie Moore and Doug Harvey were both English-speakers, although as Anglo Montrealers they understood the city's solitudes and how power was held and exercised in Duplessis's Quebec. Still, there was something fundamental at stake: a wrong needing to be made right, a respect that had finally to be shown. And it fell to him to champion, virtually alone, "his" side: he was his people's resistance leader, their archangel of revenge.

To many observers elsewhere in Canada and in professional hockey, Clarence Campbell was actually doing his best to negotiate the erratic and exasperating behaviour of a star athlete with an alarming temper and a lack of self-discipline. He was even perceived by some as being unduly lenient: only a hundred dollars for accosting a referee in a hotel lobby? Unbeknownst to all but a handful of insiders, Campbell had been pressing for a clampdown on Richard—a proper suspension, a real fine—since the late 1940s. But team owners, mindful of his drawing power, wanted him kept on the ice. Though they would never have admitted it, they had little interest in tempering the verbal, physical, even mental violence being meted out to him each night. Like a circus act in which, to the audience's fear and delight, a lion is poked until it roars, the NHL still displayed its best "theatre" in the Rocket Richard versus Everyone drama.

"If you know nothing else about the time I played," Richard would later say of this period, "know how violent the game was."

The fact was, Clarence Campbell was attempting to rein in Maurice Richard without making much effort to understand his grievances, his character, or his community. Living and working in Montreal did little to heighten Campbell's sensitivity. Operating out of the imposing stone Sun Life building, an edifice that, more than any other, represented Anglo financial dominance and smugness, and residing nearby the mentally walled ghetto of Westmount, the league president carried on both his professional duties and private life as a colonial administrator in India or Africa might have done: on site, technically, but carefully protected from undue contact with the locals by a variety of carapaces.

Richard did feel aggrieved and disrespected, and this state of mind settled over him like a cloud. He was also exhausted. His long list of chronic physical ailments was now matched by less easily itemized anxieties about his well-being, in particular the risk of permanent injury. Each night he stepped back into that coliseum and resumed playing his part in that drama. Each night he did so anticipating that he would be hacked and harassed, and be obliged—out of pride, a temper that flared too high too fast—to fight back. Men of his time, be they war vets or athletes in duress, rarely had nervous breakdowns. Instead, they were just chronically sleepless and restless, in a bad mood, not quite themselves. In a way, Richard was like a soldier, expected to do battle day in, day out, whether or not he was steeled for another conflict. Never was it a question of courage or heart; no one doubted his reserves of those qualities. The query concerned his balance, his ability to keep things in perspective, to channel his anger on ice and, of late, off it as well.

At home, he remained the same mild parent to his expanding brood. They were shortly to number seven— Huguette, Maurice Jr., Norman, André, Suzanne, Polo, and Jean—and at each birth their father wept, unashamed of feeling and showing such primal emotion. He was also still a loving, if frequently agitated, husband to Lucille. At church, too, Maurice Richard showed no signs of mental upheaval. He escorted his family to Mass most Sundays. The Richards were a handsome and exemplary Catholic clan, a decent-sized *revanche des berceaux*, the priestly admonition to the French-

Canadian flock to be fruitful and multiply, to keep the race strong on that continent of *les Anglais*. At Mass the Rocket even turned properly supplicant, kneeling when others knelt and praying on command, receiving the host—the body of Christ—on his tongue, humbled before the priest, before God, and then making the sign of the cross, just as he did before stepping into the ice before each period.

"He's supposed to be so hard," Lucille Richard told a journalist, "but you should see him at home. He's so gentle and kind, so good to the kids. Too good, I tell him." Good to them, and to her, adoring her, buying her coats and cars, taking her to nice restaurants, and to Florida in the off-season. Knowing how much she worried as well, he would call her from the dressing room if he left a road game early because of injury. Away from Montreal, he liked to talk to Lucille every day, even just a few words. She understood and loved him.

But neither the love of Lucille Richard and his children, nor his faith, nor even the much-heralded arrival of six-foot-three, 205-pound Jean "Le Gros Bill" Béliveau in the fall of 1954 (his first full season with the Habs) could alleviate the psychic pressure Maurice Richard was under. He always said that he lived for hockey, and thought about little else. What he meant was that he lived to play hockey for the Montreal

Canadiens and, in effect, for French Canada. That was a far bigger, more difficult master to please, its own needs hard to define, and fast shifting.

It took another Anglo Montrealer, novelist Hugh MacLennan, writing in *Saturday Night* in January 1955, to identify the stakes and frame the gathering narrative. "Every great player must expect to be marked closely, but for ten years the Rocket has been systematically heckled by rival coaches who knew intuitively that nobody can be more easily taken advantage of than a genius. Richard," MacLennan wrote, "can stand any amount of roughness that comes naturally with the game, but after a night in which he has been cynically tripped, slashed, held, boarded and verbally insulted by lesser men he is apt to go wild. His rage is curiously impersonal—an explosion against frustration itself." The novelist, whose empathy and identification with French Canadians had informed his 1944 novel *Two Solitudes,* still could not fully cross this cultural, linguistic, or perhaps class divide. "Owing to the way in which he has been (so they think) persecuted"—the "they" being, presumably, French Canadians—"he has imperceptibly become the focus of the persecution anxieties latent in a minority people. Not even the fact that he is loved and admired almost equally by English-speaking Montrealers can modify the profound self-

identification of loyal *Canadiens* with this singular man."
Maurice Richard, MacLennan claimed with the awe of a
sociologist describing a Stone Age society, "has the status
with some people in Quebec not that much below that of a
tribal God, and I doubt if even he realizes how much of what
he stands for in the public mind is only indirectly connect-
ed with the game he plays."

ON MARCH 13, 1955, the Canadiens were in Boston for the
second half of a late-season series with the Bruins. The game
the night before had been rough, and Richard had hurt his
back after being checked into a goalpost. The Habs were
playoff bound again, battling Detroit for top of the stand-
ings and home ice advantage. As per the norm of recent
years, he had been barely holding it together all season,
breaking the front teeth of one player with his stick and then
slapping the linesman who restrained him. His penalty total
for the 1954–55 campaign wasn't only a personal high, it
was the highest in the entire NHL. But he had also netted
his four-hundredth goal, and was three games away from
winning his first scoring title (his own young teammates,
Bernie "Boom Boom" Geoffrion and Jean Béliveau, trailed
him). Tonight, however, Richard was out of sorts, in no
small part from having to suffer the train ride down from

Montreal with a sore back. Winning the individual scoring title mattered to him, as did the money: a $1,000 bonus from the league, plus another $1,000 from the Canadiens. With his salary at $15,000, the bonuses would be welcome, especially to Lucille, who handled the family finances.

With the game locked up and just six minutes left, Bruins defenceman Hal Laycoe clipped him across the side of the head with his stick. Laycoe was called for a penalty but Richard, incensed that the Boston player would risk ending his season with a skull fracture for no good reason, rubbed his scalp, his eyes gone black with fury. When his fingers came up bloody—he would require five stitches later—he skated over and, using both hands, brought his stick down over Laycoe's head and shoulders with full force. (The Bruin, who wore glasses, partially absorbed the blow with his arms.) A linesman, knowing Richard's propensity for repeat attacks, confiscated his weapon and restrained him. He broke away, grabbed another player's stick, and cracked it over Laycoe's back. This time, the official wrestled him to the ice. A teammate helped free him, and Richard, up on his feet, first punched the official in the face and then, finding Laycoe again (minus the glasses), blackened his eye with a string of quick jabs. Though it had been fifteen years since his last boxing lesson he remained a solid fighter, always ready to throw the first punch and rarely losing a fair contest.

As the crowd howled, Richard was escorted off the ice. In the dressing room after the game, two officers from the Boston police attempted to arrest him for assault and battery with a dangerous weapon. Wisely, coach Dick Irvin barred them at the door; extracting his athlete from a police station once charges had been laid would have been much more difficult, and could have affected Richard's future ability to cross the border to play. Only after the Bruins general manager assured police that the NHL would handle the matter did authorities agree to let the Rocket go home to Canada.

His outburst, and the attempt to arrest him, granted Clarence Campbell all the justification he needed. The league president called for a morning hearing into the incident in his office three days later. Richard agreed not to speak in public until then. In turn, Campbell promised to keep an open mind, hear his side of the story, and then decide on a penalty. The team and the city waited nervously for March 16. Ten men in suits sat around a small table in the Sun Life building: Richard, Irvin, and Kenny Reardon, now the team's assistant manager; the referees who had officiated the Boston game and their boss; Hal Laycoe and his boss, the owner of the Bruins; and Campbell. It all seemed respectful, the athletes being treated as adults, with Maurice Richard—the one person actually on trial—allowed to explain himself, albeit in English, the only language the president spoke. The meeting lasted almost three hours, and then Campbell informed the parties that he would deliberate. Dick Irvin didn't agree with some of the things the referees told the president; they sounded like what he wanted to hear to justify plans already made. He left the hearing worried it had been fixed.

Irvin was right. Clarence Campbell had flown in secret to New York two days earlier and met with league owners to ask their support in suspending Richard until the following autumn. Media coverage of his meltdown in Boston had been widespread. Only three games remained in the regular season, meaning little or no revenue would be lost if the Rocket did not play. The owners agreed, with Conn Smythe of the Maple Leafs in particular taking pleasure in jamming up the Canadiens' playoff hopes.

On the afternoon of March 16, the NHL president told the media that, given Richard's "pattern of conduct," the "time for leniency or probation is past." Openly questioning his mental state—"Whether this type of conduct is the product of temperamental instability or wilful defiance doesn't matter"—Campbell suspended Maurice Richard for the remainder of the season and the playoffs.

Children defy adults; slaves defy masters. Unstable people are not heroes and leaders, and in the 1950s they were shameful secrets, swiftly institutionalized, chemically sedated, and then often forgotten. Had Clarence Campbell prepared his comments more carefully, he might have reconsidered ascribing Richard's on-ice rages to psychological factors unrelated to anything he had experienced as a hockey player. Had he possessed an intuitive connection with French Quebec, or been surrounded by advisers with greater awareness of it, even simply of the Hugh MacLennan "persecution anxieties latent in a minority people" variety, he might have confined his remarks to the violent actions that had warranted such a punishment. (Today, Richard would almost certainly be tried for assault for what he did to Hal Laycoe.) Or not: in his characterization of Maurice Richard, the president of the NHL, true to the cliché of the aloof Anglo overlord, betrayed the condescension he not-so-secretly felt for the denizens of the city in which he lived and worked, right down to their chosen son, officially the greatest hockey player on the planet, but in Campbell's view just another emotional, self-indulgent French Canadian.

That same night the league's top official began hearing from those same denizens. People called his office, threatening to bomb it and to kill him. "Tell Campbell I'm an undertaker and he'll be needing me in a few days," went one message. "Simply revolting" and "a screaming injustice" announced the populist *Montréal-Matin* the next morning. What Clarence Campbell had said about Maurice Richard was "absolutely false" and a "flagrant lie," and the penalty, ostensibly meted out to an individual, was actually being shared by the public. "This is how we would like to see him," ran the caption of a crude cartoon published elsewhere. It showed Campbell's head on a platter, dripping blood. If there was to be violence against the president, it wouldn't go unchallenged: former army mates from elsewhere in the country called his office as well, offering to come to Quebec to back up their commander.

March 17 was St Patrick's Day, but in Montreal, according to one radio call-in show, it was "Blow Up the Sun Life Building Day." A decisive home game was scheduled for 8:30 with Detroit, a physically intimidating team starring Gordie Howe and the still "Terrible" Ted Lindsay, with the season championship in play. Despite the cold, protestors were gathering outside the Forum as early as noon, carrying placards announcing *"Vive Richard"* and *"Richard persécuté"*

("Richard is being persecuted"), *"À bas Campbell"* ("Down with Campbell") and *"Injustice au Canada français"* ("Injustice against French Canada"). In the afternoon a copy of a photograph of Maurice Richard was plastered on bulletin boards outside the arena. The upcoming April issue of the American magazine *Sport* was running a piece on the Habs, and the distributor had made up posters encouraging hockey fans to "Read this month's *Sport:* Montreal's Flying Frenchmen. Now on Sale." Richard had sat for a photo shoot earlier in the winter.

The image they had chosen was arresting. It was also strangely familiar. The Rocket, shown from the midsection, wore his vivid red uniform, his sweat-glazed skin shiny in the photographer's light. The camera had caught him with his eyes rolling heavenward and his right shoulder lowered. His stick, meanwhile, cut across his torso at a 120-degree angle. Art lovers outside the Forum might have stopped in their tracks at the congruencies between the photo and the seventeenth-century Luca Giordano painting *The Martyrdom of Saint Sebastian.* Sebastian was a Roman praetorian allegedly put to death by the emperor for his Christian views in the third century AD, and had long been a symbol of Christ-like martyrdom. In dozens of paintings from the Renaissance onward, he was represented tied to a pole with an arrow shot through his upper torso, right to left, gazing at heaven in acceptance of his status as sacrificial lamb. In the *Sport* portrait, Saint Maurice seemed to gaze up to heaven for support as well, his stick a kind of arrow running through him.

A visual coincidence, nothing more, the photo was of a psychological piece with the aroused passions that night. (Earlier, a cartoonist had depicted a boy dreaming of Richard as Superman, complete with a cape and an "S" on his chest—a more obvious, "waking" analogy.) With darkness fallen on March 17, but the game still two hours away, trucks dislodged squads of young men in windbreakers in a park across from the Forum. Montreal police associated the garments with freelance anarchists, many linked to motorcycle gangs, who liked to cause trouble around the city. Radio stations set up mobile units nearby, broadcasting live, their remarks ranging from the bitter to the inflammatory. By 8:30, with the puck about to be dropped inside, announcements that the game was sold out didn't budge the crowd of six hundred milling around the main entrance. "We don't want seats," they chanted. "We want Campbell."

Midway through the first period, with Richard seated quietly near the goal judge at one end, well away from the benches and dressing rooms, the league president arrived with his secretary and fiancée, Phyllis King. Clarence Campbell was rarely late to games, and by appearing during the action he drew accidental attention to himself as he climbed the stairs to his customary seat. Word of his presence climbed too, up out of the affluent red section to the proletarian blue section, either seated or standing. From on high poured the catcalls: *"Va-t'en! Va-t'en!"* and "Get lost!" The Canadiens, clearly undone by the off-ice drama, quickly fell behind by two goals. Boot rubbers, programs, tomatoes, eggs, and even a pickled pig's foot soon rained down on Campbell. A few projectiles hit the fifty-year-old, and each time he calmly stood up to wipe the debris from his shoulders, widening himself as a target and inflaming the mischief-makers.

Two more Detroit goals had the same effect, as the game slipped away before the first period was even ended. During intermission, with Campbell under the impression it was prudent to stay in his seat—normally he sat with the referees between periods—the situation further deteriorated. Ushers were positioned to protect the expensive seats from interlopers, but two young men got past the loose security and spoke their minds. The first squashed a tomato against the president's chest and rubbed it in ("to make Campbell's soup," he later said). The second extended one hand and tried slugging him with the other. Campbell was expecting the punch and deflected most of the blows. Some eighty police officers were on duty at the Forum, but they were pre-occupied with the crowd outside. Sensing his vulnerability, dozens more young men descended from the cheap seats, intending the *maudit Anglais* real harm.

A homemade smoke bomb may have saved Clarence Campbell from being more seriously assaulted. It landed twenty-five feet away, sending up plumes of yellow smoke. The bomb, which contained a canister of tear gas—he rec-ognized the smell at once from the war—left people choking and covering their eyes and noses with scarves and handker-chiefs. Finally, the NHL president retreated to the security of the first-aid centre under the stands. Richard, it so hap-pened, also slipped out of the rink to the centre, but into a different room, unaware his nemesis was nearby. As such, the two "players" in the drama, the cause and effect of the now-apparent crisis, were out of the picture. With patrons fleeing the sections near the bomb, the head of the Montreal fire department demanded the Forum be cleared. Consenting, Campbell sent the Red Wings coach a note say-ing that the game had been forfeited to them, and he could take his team "on its way anytime now."

Suspending play and expelling the crowd from the building drove an additional fourteen thousand people, all agitated, many livid, a few with stinging eyes and coughs, into those same streets. Though maybe half did proceed home, enough stayed to swell the protest, then still as much an anarchic party as a riot. Suddenly, the Forum windows were being smashed and a bullet mysteriously fired. The police, now reinforced to more than two hundred officers, resolved to funnel the crowd east along St. Catherine Street, away from Westmount but back toward the downtown along the city's principal shopping strip. Their decision transformed protestors into a mob. Young men began setting cars on fire. They rocked streetcars and destroyed letter boxes and newspaper stands. Store windows were smashed using bottles, blocks of ice, and bricks from a construction site. A giant effigy of Richard, brought out on earlier occasions to celebrate his achievements, now appeared on the back of a truck, a grinning, ghoulish puppet trailing the rioters down the street and flitting in and out of sight in the light of the street lamps. The participants held up the same picket signs declaring "Long live Richard" and "We want Richard," along with "Stupid puppet Campbell" and "Our national sport destroyed," especially if one of the dozens of newspaper cameramen was nearby. But the placards, written in both languages, went largely unread in the dark.

Concerns about fairness and pride gave way to baser matters, and by the end of the five-hour rampage the rioters, the majority of whom were young francophone men from working-class areas, were looting shops, paying special attention to the window displays of jewellers. By 4 A.M., when the riot finally exhausted itself, there were minor injuries among the police, a hundred arrests and eighty indictments, and major property damage along a five-kilometre stretch of St. Catherine.

Maurice Richard, furious that the game had been forfeited to Detroit, drove back to Ahuntsic at 10 P.M., leaving the downtown behind him. He only heard news of the mayhem on the car radio. When manager Frank Selke called his house at midnight, asking him to return to the arena to help disperse the crowd, he declined, worried they might instead try hoisting him on their shoulders and parading him through the city. He kept track of events into the early morning from his living room.

The next day Mayor Jean Drapeau assigned blame for the riot on Clarence Campbell for showing up at the Forum. "It would not be necessary to give too many such decisions to kill hockey in Montreal," Drapeau said ominously. From the Sun Life building Campbell defended himself, saying that he would never back down to "severe hoodlums," and that "the league governors have all called me and congratulated me for attending last night's game." City police, meanwhile, unsure of what darkness would bring that coming night, were reported in the daily tabloids to be debating the wisdom of introducing martial law. Implored by the team management and by close friends to help calm the situation, a shaken but still reluctant Richard drove back to the Forum for an evening broadcast. Dressed in an elegant grey suit and tie, he sat behind a desk set up inside the Habs dressing room, a field of microphones, each bearing the station call number—CFCF, CKAC, CJAD, CJMS—on the desk, a television camera farther back. In his naturally quiet, subdued voice, he read a brief statement, first in French and then in English. Richard, who had written the statement himself in both languages, called for restraint. "Because I always try so hard to win and had my troubles in Boston, I was suspended," he said in the English version. "At playoff time it hurts not to be in the game with the boys. However, I want to do what is good for the people of Montreal and my team. So that no further harm will be done, I would like everyone to get behind the team and to help the boys win from the New York Rangers and Detroit." Then, as if sensing his absence would be fatal to the team's chances in spring 1955, he said: "I will take my punishment and come back next year to help the club and the younger players to win the Cup."

Any whisper of resurrecting the riot for a second night, or of exacting revenge on Clarence Campbell, ended with those simple words. Montreal heeded his command.

Richard's final remark of the broadcast, predicting a 1956 Stanley Cup with a team led by the younger players, came true on two levels. Though the Canadiens reached the finals without him that spring, they lost a close series four games to three to the same Red Wings. In the absence of Richard, however, those youngsters—Geoffrion, Béliveau, Dickie Moore—stepped up, gaining valuable experience and confidence. To his own chagrin, the charismatic Geoffrion, who had worshipped Richard since he was a boy and whose nickname "Boom Boom" related to his pioneering of the slapshot, overtook the suspended Rocket to win the scoring title by a point. Geoffrion had done everything he could *not* to score, but still became the target of hate mail for daring to surpass his mentor.

"On a tué Mon Frère Richard" ran the title of the *Le Devoir* piece by André Laurendeau, associate editor-in-chief. The headline—"Richard, My Brother, Has Been Killed"— echoed an earlier incident in the evolution of French-Canadian nationalism: the trial and execution of Métis

leader Louis Riel in 1885. Upon hearing that Riel had been hanged in Manitoba, Quebec premier Honoré Mercier famously said, "Riel, our brother, is dead," bannering under one family roof the mixed-blood Métis of Manitoba with the French of Quebec. To associate a visionary political leader like Riel, who had been executed for treason, with a hockey player suspended for a few games for on-ice violence was, on one level, absurd and self-dramatizing. But the gifted Laurendeau, at various stages of his career a novelist, playwright, television commentator, journalist, and politician, seized the narrative moment with a propagandist's sharp eye and pen. "French-Canadian nationalism seems to have taken refuge in hockey," he began. "The crowd that roared its anger on Thursday night was not driven only by sporting rivalry or by a sense of the injustice committed against its idol. It was a people frustrated, protesting against its fate." Maurice Richard was a "national hero" and Clarence Campbell an embodiment of "all the real or imaginary adversaries that this little people has encountered." Admitting the comparison with Riel was extreme—"Today's death sentence was a symbolic one"—Laurendeau insisted that the "Richard Riot," as it was already being called, was in its own way as monumental as the hanging of Louis Riel. "But one brief flare-up has revealed what has been slumbering beneath the apparent indifference and the long passivity of the French Canadians."

Or so, the editorial suggested, nationalist intellectuals like the writers and editors of *Le Devoir* were hoping. They wanted to construct and direct a new historic narrative, and wasted no time in casting the riot as a deeper reflection of a people, a nation, playing out its identity.

Like the agitations of Pierre Trudeau and Gérard Pelletier in the journal *Cité Libre,* the cerebral rallying cries of a tiny, elite newspaper hardly registered among those small "frustrated people" who had, by André Laurendeau's own uneasy admission, behaved in a manner that was "aggressive and incoherent" in the city streets after the game. More audible to them were the songs that appeared on the airwaves in Quebec, and, notably, the rest of Canada, within a month of the riot. "The Saga of Maurice Richard," written by the country band Bob Hill and his Canadian Country Boys and set to a nineteenth-century Irish melody, told the tale in lively, verbose English:

> Says Campbell, "Young man, that stick in your hand
>   has put you in trouble, by gar
> Though you needed five stitches, you're too big for
>   your britches

Just who do you think you are?
Now you've done this before, and you've made me
    quite sore
And although you are a great star
You're through for the year, do I make myself clear
Mister Maurice, 'the Rocket' Richard?"

In Quebec, Oscar Thiffault's "Le Rocket Richard" was also set to another popular folk melody, this one French-Canadian: *"C'est Maurice Richard qui est si populaire / "C'est Maurice Richard qui score tout le temps,"* went the singalong chorus: "Maurice Richard is the most popular / Richard who scores all the time." Thiffault told his saga in brief—*Par un dimanche au soir en jouant à Boston / Vous auriez dû voir les fameux coups d'baton* ("One Sunday night playing Boston / You should have seen the famous stick battles")—and then moved onto a tribal defence of the hero:

Y a été suspendu
On a été chanceux qu'il ne sois pas vendu
Comme un bon Canadien y a accepté son sort
Il reviendra compter pour le Canadien encore.

(They suspended him

We were lucky they didn't sell him
Like a good Canadian he took it like a man
He'll be back to score again.)

These popular, and populist, songs, while written in different languages, addressed the same constituency: "regular"
people living in every city and town in "both" Canadas.
Maurice Richard may not have been aware of it—though his
sense of isolation was powerful and honestly felt, it was also
unfounded—but the appeal of his play, and his character,
went well beyond Quebec and French Canada. To an
admirer in Alberta or the Yukon, he was not so much the
unofficial leader of an oppressed minority who had been
unjustly punished by a callow Anglo overlord. Rather, he
was a great hockey player and an intense, appealing man
who inspired a heroic squad that was, for most Canadians
outside Ontario, "their" national team. Even among French
Montrealers, whether working-class or the elite of
Outremont, the narrative wasn't uniform. For Duplessis, he
was the easily manipulated hero of the "real" people, themselves conveniently silent. For *Le Devoir,* he was a helpful
symbol and a potential catalyst: just what their nationalist
project needed. But for many others, most notably members
of the *rouge* tradition in Quebec, a federalist position that

went virtually missing during *La grande noirceur,* he was something else again: *un bon Canadien,* as Oscar Thiffault put it in "Le Rocket Richard."

As for Maurice Richard himself, there are indications that he wasn't especially confident of his political positions, and would have preferred not to have been asked about them at all. Once the events of March 1955 were adorned with his name, his own views were suddenly, and permanently, immaterial. What *others* believed he should be, could be, had to be, for historical and political reasons, now mattered. There was a riot going on in Quebec, and history—one, two, three competing versions of it—too long dormant, was suddenly on the move.

CHAPTER SIX

Dynasty

I still dream about it at night.
MAURICE RICHARD ON THE "RICHARD RIOT"

Much changed for Maurice Richard that tumultuous spring. Not for Richard the quiescent symbol or catalyst of change, but for Richard the banged-up veteran athlete and mentally drained Montrealer. In April, with the season done, he and Lucille packed their car and joined the annual armada of Canadiens players driving down to Florida. Veterans Doug Harvey, Butch Bouchard, and Ken Mosdell were accompanied by the gregarious Bernie Geoffrion. For two weeks the couples ate good food and drank lots of beer, went deep-sea fishing and played shuffleboard. If they were recognized on the beach, it was usually by fellow French Canadians, likewise in flight from the persistent Montreal late winter, who stopped them to get their pictures taken and chat. If Richard was alone with Lucille, or with Bouchard or Geoffrion, they would naturally slip into their first language, but otherwise conversations were in English, as was any television viewing, movie watching, or newspaper buying—although wily vendors stocked Montreal papers on sale a day or two late. This was the United States, after all, but for francophone athletes it was also the "rest of North America," a vast, only minimally differentiated geographic reality in their lives. There was equally no forgetting their status on a beach in Fort Lauderdale or a sandy strand in Prince Edward County, Ontario; there was little to set apart a night in a hotel, and a game in a rink, in Chicago or Detroit from one in Toronto. About Canada, most were familiar with only Toronto-the-Good, and maybe Ottawa-the-Dreary, with the occasional fishing trip taking them over into the Restigouche region of New Brunswick. Knowing Toronto best—the bellicose, charmless Conn Smythe and abusive fans in Maple Leaf Gardens, the flatlined thrills of an overnight stay in a city where sidewalks rolled up at sunset—hardly encouraged a wider curiosity about what kind of country lay west of the Great Lakes.

On his return to Montreal in May, a revived Richard was implicated in an important coaching decision. He had only ever played for one man professionally. After eleven years together, his relationship with Dick Irvin was seamless, each knowing what the other wanted with only occasional need for words. (At the start, they'd communicated through accidental interpreter Butch Bouchard; for the last half decade, Richard's English had allowed for direct conversations.) Irvin certainly understood Maurice Richard's gift and the explosiveness of his moods, and how to get the best out of him, especially in pressure situations, where the coach never hesitated to use psychology to push his buttons, regardless if he was already in a blind fury or cut and bleeding. Dick Irvin was himself a scrapper, accustomed from decades on the prairies and an early career with the Black Hawks to the slower, more physical hockey played elsewhere. Though he now oversaw a squad increasingly filled with gifted skaters and stickhandlers, he still opted too often to grind it out with teams like the Red Wings. Canadiens manager Frank Selke, aware that Maurice Richard was close to burnt-out, doubted Irvin would be willing or able to rethink how he used the veteran star. For everyone's sake, the fiery coach had to go. Offered a job-for-life in management, Irvin opted instead to return to Chicago.

In an inspired move, the team brought Toe Blake back from seven years in exile, during which the Rocket's former linemate had evolved into a skilled leader behind the bench of a string of Habs' minor-league affiliates. On learning Blake was a candidate, Richard advocated for him, even threatening to quit if another candidate was chosen instead. Part of his reason for wanting the classy Blake was his fluency in French. Raised near Sudbury, Ontario, by a French mother and English father, Blake spoke both languages with ease. Richard and others, believing it long past due, had secretly advocated for a French-Canadian coach. During the summer, Selke, Blake, and Richard met, and Blake told Richard that from now on he should leave the rough stuff to the younger players: no more fist fights with guys a decade his junior. Forget about the past, he told him. It's the future—and you—that we're concerned about. They eventually appointed him team captain, sweet recognition for a player who, while long acknowledged as the engine of the Habs, had also been presumed too volatile to perform that function. Now they trusted he would be calmer, if never quite statesmanlike.

Surrounding him starting that fall was a team so deep and varied in talent it could play anyone's style, slow or fast, grinding or skating. From the dazzling and innovative Jacques Plante in goal to the dominating defenceman Doug Harvey and forwards Béliveau, Geoffrion, and Moore, the Montreal Canadiens of the 1955–60 period were a powerhouse. "Then there's team spirit," Frank Selke would later say of the squad, his language authentic to the times, "and the strength that comes from two or more racial units on the club, each with a different approach mentally to the game. The player of English or German or Polish descent has the inborn urge to drive right in, to smash his way along. On the other hand, there's the Gallic spirit of our French-Canadian players. They like to set up plays in almost dramatic fashion by passing the puck. They're the artists of the game."

Once his close friend Bouchard retired in 1956, Maurice Richard graduated to being the oldest player on the squad. At nineteen, another Richard was also the youngest member. He was Henri, Maurice's kid brother. The addition of the swift centre made further psychic sense: now there was even more Richard to go around, lifting part of the burden from the famous elder's shoulders. As did Maurice fourteen years before, the five-foot-seven Henri arrived in the NHL without a word of English. Also like Maurice, he signed his first contract without being able to read it. He did not ask for, nor was he offered, his older sibling's help with the negotiation, and signed for three seasons for around $5,500 each, a third what his brother was being paid. Like, it seemed, all the Richards, Henri's natural reticence ran deep, and aside from posing for a photograph together, the brothers did not exchange a word during their first season as teammates, with the teenager soon known as the "Pocket Rocket" sticking close to the younger players and leaving Maurice to the company of the veterans. "I'd hardly ever see him," Henri Richard told a reporter of growing up in the Rocket's afterglow. "He was like any other guy."

For five straight seasons the Habs coached by Toe Blake and captained (for four) by Maurice Richard weren't only unbeatable, they weren't seriously challenged. The hoisting of the Stanley Cup each spring became so routine that city officials began announcing the parade would follow the "usual route." Such dominance was without precedent in professional sports, and helped consolidate the notion of a franchise to the championship born, with the 1955–60 Montreal Canadiens as the model. (Only the New York Yankees in baseball were then a rival paradigm of excellence; in the 1960s, the Boston Celtics in basketball would emerge as a third.) Their captain had two solid seasons, of thirty-eight and thirty-three goals, followed by three limited years, missing much of the '57–58 campaign and close to half of the next one with injuries. Goal-scoring totals of just fifteen, seventeen, and nineteen trailed Richard to the end of the 1950s, and of his own fourth decade. By spring 1960 the great Maurice Richard was closing in on forty, an old man struggling with a young man's game.

Under Blake's stewardship, his penalty totals dropped

from the *noirceur* years until he was, if never predictable or gentlemanly, then unlikely to explode. He saw less need to brandish his stick as sabre and got into fewer and fewer fights. Opposition players, too, stopped taking him on, either because he was Maurice Richard, at once a living records book and, as of August 1957, the oldest player in the NHL, or because other Habs, younger, bigger, were not above retaliating on his behalf, without seeking his permission (which would be emphatically denied). Players still did their own fighting, whether Hart Trophy winners or journeymen, but all of a sudden trading blows with the Rocket seemed, even for the pugilists of hockey, unsportsmanlike. When the Rocket scored his five hundredth goal at the Forum at age thirty-six, the announcer had to wait for two minutes until the ovation subsided. "Canadiens goal scored by Mr. Hockey himself, Maurice Richard," he finally intoned.

Who would pick a fight with Mr. Hockey himself?

That said, Richard was no figurehead, especially come the playoffs, and no one questioned his effectiveness or relevance. In the 1958 post-season, after managing just twenty-eight regular-season games, he scored seven in a semifinals sweep of Detroit and then another four in the Stanley Cup win over Boston. "It's always the same: the unique, the inimitable Maurice Richard," a journalist wrote, granting that his playoff performances were becoming "more and more fantastic each year because the Rocket should have disappeared from the game a long time ago." He had overcome a severed Achilles tendon that year, costing him three months, and the next January, in an eerie revisiting of the injuries that had nearly scuttled his career before it started, he broke an ankle. He also fractured a cheekbone. Each time he healed, but a little more slowly, and with a little more anxiety about what the next cut or fracture might be, once confessing to the media that he was suffering nightmares in which he ended up a paraplegic, wheelchair-bound. "I've felt awful for the last three years," Richard said during one playoff run. "It's not that I'm sick, but I've been hurt so often. I just can't keep up the pace anymore."

Maurice Richard was also greying around the temples and thickening in the middle, as men of his build naturally do. Though a half-stroke slower, he remained a powerful skater, as much from force of will as leg strength. He was also still a chore to contain, sweeping in from the right side of the ice, leaning into the defender to keep him at bay, and then either cutting across the crease and jamming the puck in or else skating behind the net and emerging on the far side for a wraparound backhand. He just didn't do these things as often. Off-season training, then largely unknown in hockey, aside from playing baseball and golf and maybe lifting a few weights in the basement, might have helped. But there was no avoiding getting older, and the wear and tear. Still, there was no talk of retirement—not yet.

His dream life was certainly vivid. Nightmares of catastrophic injuries were being matched, he admitted, by occasional nocturnal reveries about the events of March 1955. "I still dream about it," Richard would later say of the riot. In a sense, the Montreal Canadiens team he was captaining must have seemed a waking dream to him. This was hockey being played at about as high and graceful a level imaginable. While no longer necessarily the centre of attention or controversy—Geoffrion and Moore scored more goals, Béliveau had more points, and lesser players fought more fights—he was the team's indisputable heart. Victories of all kinds were slowly but clearly coming in Quebec. The "Flying Frenchmen," those "artists of the game"—including Henri Richard, who quickly surpassed his brother in annual point totals—dominated the NHL, winning the scoring title or finishing near the top most years. The French language had more currency in the Habs dressing room than ever before. Even his nemesis Clarence Campbell, while still headquartered in the Sun Life building on Dorchester

Square and still comfortable awarding the Stanley Cup each spring to Captain Maurice Richard and the French-dominated Canadiens squad using only English—not one *Bonsoir mesdames et messieurs,* not one *Félicitations,* escaped his lips—had to smile for photos standing next to the Rocket, and then witness the "usual" parade along the "usual" route through the mostly French city. The league president was certainly not detecting any early warning signals about the changes about to sweep through Montreal in the new decade. He continued to see scant need to show respect to the team, the city, the culture, in that manner. But his prejudice no longer necessitated a riot: the dynastic Montreal Canadiens had dignity, power, and success—a happy waking dream for French Canadians as well.

Television made a glittering show of the *bleu, blanc, rouge.* Starting in October 1952, just a few weeks after the birth of the CBC and Radio-Canada television networks, the Habs were on TV most Saturday nights. There was *La soirée du hockey* for Quebecers who were lucky enough to own a set, and who could get a signal, and *Hockey Night in Canada* for the rest of the country. Strategies for televising the sport steadily improved throughout the 1950s. Three overhead cameras were originally employed, with a fourth introduced at ice level in 1956, allowing for more intimate coverage of play around the net. That same year a procedure was created allowing the CBC to reproduce a recording of a goal within thirty seconds of its being scored. Near "instant replay" was born. Still, many games were not covered—the inciting incident for the Richard Riot in Boston, for instance, went untelevised—and because of CBC scheduling, telecasts did not begin until 9 P.M. Even with start times at 8:30, the network was joining games in progress, a problem that wouldn't be solved for the regular season until 1968, two years after the introduction of colour.

Television also augured, slowly, the age of corporate ownership and, slower still, salaries for players more in keeping with their value. In 1958 the Molson family bought controlling interest in the Canadiens, and almost immediately used this base to acquire part of the *Hockey Night in Canada* sponsorship for their breweries. By 1963 their support share equalled that of the original sponsor, Imperial Oil.

Along with the action, TV cameras, staging pre-game encounters with the players along the boards, captured the princely Jean Béliveau and boyish Bernie Geoffrion, along with the bland, priestly visage of Jacques Plante, now hidden during games behind the first-ever goalie mask. With his groomed hair and dark gaze, his wincing smile and always full set of white teeth, Richard needed no introduction. But he had also learned over the years how to best present him-self on camera: keep still and show his profile, hold his smile. With age, too, he was becoming more distinguished, and with consecutive championships and a young team that could now carry him, and not the other way round, his body language was relaxed, almost—*almost,* for a naturally anx-ious man—at ease.

Traceable on his face might have been the relief of some-one living downstream of a psychological dam that had finally burst, relieving impossible private pressure. The repercussions of the Richard Riot may still have been gath-ering cultural and political force—by now there were two novels that used the riot in their plots, including 1956's *Les inutiles (The Useless Ones)* by Eugène Cloutier, concerning two escapees from a mental institution who find themselves at the Forum on that fateful night, where "a new civilization was on the march, one that could not be foretold"—but the positive effects on its namesake were already evident.

October 1952, the birth of televised hockey, had occurred at the halfway point of Richard's career, and on the eve of its most tumultuous, and then most triumphant, periods. His five-goal playoff game against Toronto in 1944, his fifty-goals-in-fifty-games achievement the following year, the three early Stanley Cups, and the magnificent 1946–47 season that saw him awarded his only Hart Trophy as league MVP: all survive only as black-and-white photographs and newspaper clippings, and in partially preserved radio accounts. Limited TV coverage of regular-season games outside Montreal and Toronto, where he tended to erupt most violently, meant that mass audiences saw little of what was most astounding, thrilling, and often disconcerting about the younger Maurice Richard. Headlong rushes and dazzling goals, ferocious stick duels and fearsome fist fights, meltdowns in penalty boxes and tussles with referees were, from the start, dramatic tales told live by ebullient radio commentators, retold swiftly by journalists paid to declaim in forty-eight-point headlines, and then retold again and again by eyewitnesses at Madison Square Garden and Boston Garden, the Forum and Maple Leaf Gardens, and by the people *those* people told about the unbelievable things the Rocket had done on the ice that night. Iconic photos survived, imperfect, irregularly lit, and occasionally surreal: his handshake with Boston goalie Jim "Sugar" Henry and his awkward leap into Elmer Lach after scoring in a play-off game (he broke Lach's nose in his excitement). Plus the very rare and special image that did justice to the Rocket's intensity and passion, those headlight-wide black eyes, no less frantic than they were fierce. But that was all.

The earlier Maurice Richard, in short, had been only partially preserved. Better: technological limitations had cast him for eternity in a sepia light, one comfortable with gaps in the historic record, allowing plenty of space for legend, myth, even social and political needs, to have an impact on perception and memory. Being pre-TV probably worked in his favour, editing out the shocking visual evidence of his lack of restraint, his disturbing capacity for violence. The older, slower, more statesmanlike Richard, in contrast, was soon familiar to Canadian television viewers, coast to coast, and he was both less problematic as a sports icon and more widely appealing. (He was also no longer the silent, embarrassed young athlete during televised interviews in English, speaking it fluently, if with his usual reserve.) That older Richard certainly fit better with the dynastic Montreal Canadiens, now almost above the mayhem of the bad old days; he may also have been what French Canada required on the eve of its own forthcoming assertions about identity and destiny.

Richard's standing as a commodity was also being transformed. He continued to endorse an array of products for the Quebec and Canadian markets. His name and face appeared on everything from Bee Hive syrup (*"Suivez l'exemple de Maurice Richard—régalez-vous avec le Sirop Bee*

Hive sur du pain, des céréales, et des crêpes") and a line of jerseys and sweaters *("Salopette Maurice Richard Gilet Sport")* in French, Vitalis hair tonic ("My hair shapes up like a league leader after the Vitalis '60-Second Workout!'") and Prest-O-Lite Hi-Level Battery ("Maurice Richard says, 'I add water only three times a year'") in English, and even a shaving cream marketed to the Spanish-speaking public *("El Campeón de 'hockey' Maurice Richard se afeita mejor con Williams porque Williams contiene lanolina confortante")*. But new to his endorsements were ads or media-generated images showing him as parent and mentor, presenting that avuncular, TV-friendly, almost "civilian" Maurice Richard, one with his society's deeper needs in mind.

Several related to a pastime he was not previously known for: reading. In one advertisement, for a series of books for children, he was depicted reading to one of his sons—on the ice, no less, with Jean Béliveau looking on. In another, from 1958, a portfolio of photos showed Richard watching another of his boys read a book aloud, and helping his children do their homework. "Next to goals, or perhaps on a par with scoring," the profile reported, "Richard is a sucker for children. He will referee a kids game at the drop of a hat if he's available and he willingly and eagerly makes hospital appearances whenever he can." It was true: he adored children, most especially his own seven; he loved how he could be soft and tender around them and not worry about being sufficiently tough or grand. But the photos were also part of a campaign to cast him in that softer light.

A 1959 cover of *Maclean's* helped explain the campaign. The drawing depicts Richard, dashing in a suit and with a five o'clock shadow on his cheeks, signing autographs for a scrum of adoring boys at a hockey banquet. Shown clearly, and purposefully, is the program naming the banquet as *Les Loisirs de l'Immaculée Conception,* linking it to a Catholic church and a genial priest seated at the head table. As in the ads for books, Richard here was depicted not as a salesman or huckster, feeding off his fame to sell pretty much any product that would pay his fee, but as a fine example of a citizen and a community leader.

Or a politician? In fall 1959, the privately apolitical Maurice Richard could have easily won the provincial seat in his riding in north Montreal for whatever party he chose to stand for, likely without campaigning. Alternatively, he could have secured a federal seat in the next election without much more difficulty, and sat in Parliament in Ottawa. Along with the eternally ruling Duplessis, he remained one of the two famous "Maurices" from a decade earlier. Since then, too, he had both emphatically done one thing—won an additional five Stanley Cups—and been credited with another, less tangible accomplishment: somehow triggering a populist nationalist movement.

But these achievements, real or notional, hadn't altered how he viewed himself as a professional athlete. The idea of fraternizing with "enemy" players, with whom he had been doing battle for almost twenty years, was still anathema. As did so many athletes of his era, Richard saw himself as a member of a clan, and other teams as opposing clans, with the fight being both multi-generational and to the death. Nor had his thinking about the business of hockey much evolved. In 1956 a group of players, once again under the stewardship of his archnemesis Ted Lindsay, tried forming a union, in no small part to address the emergence of television as a lucrative revenue stream for the sport. Even with his teammate Doug Harvey on board, Richard was reluctant to do more than endorse the initiative in pursed-lipped silence. (At least he didn't oppose it, as did another front-rank player: Gordie Howe, his rival in being an on-ice lion and off-ice mouse.) Clarence Campbell still spoke of any agitations by the athletes as impertinent and even treasonous. Maurice Richard, whose endorsement would have been huge, kept his mouth shut while Campbell and the team owners harassed, manipulated, lied to, and finally punished the instigators, with Red Wings boss James Adams first smearing Lindsay's reputation and then effectively ending his career by trading him to the Black Hawks. Once the Detroit team buckled under the pressure and withdrew their support for the players' association, it quickly folded.

Later, Richard would claim he had kept silent in order to not seem superior to the younger players on the Habs. But the reality was, or remained, that even in the glorious twilight of his glorious career, with little to lose and a potential legacy to pass on to those younger athletes, who deserved better salaries and pensions than his generation had procured for themselves, he was instinctively diffident around his Anglo bosses—the residue, perhaps, of growing up a small person in that manufactured vision of a quiet, familial, Catholic Quebec. It was a vision Richard happened to cherish, a reflection of the moral standards he lived his own life by, and so he found it impossible to challenge. Regardless, had he wished, he could have gone into politics, almost certainly for Duplessis's Union Nationale, and would undoubtedly have represented that Quebec with dignity.

But the autumn of 1959 unfolded in a way that soon ruled out this post-hockey option. Fifteen years of continuous government by Maurice Duplessis ended on September 7, when the premier died of a cerebral hemorrhage at age sixty-nine. His successor, Paul Sauvé, went to work almost the next morning attacking the corruption that had flourished under *le chef,* as well as addressing the neglected education and medical systems. The progressive Sauvé, who had waited patiently in the margins of the Union Nationale for his chance, did extraordinary work in his first hundred days in office. But that is all he was given; on January 2, 1960, the fifty-three-year-old succumbed to a heart attack. A new election would not be called until the following summer, but an era, an ethos—the Quebec, in effect, of Maurice Richard—was collapsing.

At almost exactly the same time, a kind of death watch for Richard's hockey career began in earnest. The cover of one magazine that fall offered a drawing of the Rocket and the line *Est-ce sa dernière saison?* ("Is this his final season?"). "There are men upon whom, from birth, lies the curse of greatness," began a grandiose essay in *Le Petit Journal* about his imminent departure. It portrayed him as the solitary hero, his lonely fate to be an agent of political transformation. "Almost always misunderstood by their contemporaries," the essayist wrote of this kind of hero, such men "streak across the sky of history like meteors…. They themselves do not know who they are, nor the roads their fate will follow. In the rise and dizzying fall of their lives they barely touch the real world."

Less swooning, but still capturing the magnitude of his pending exit from hockey, was the cover of the March 21, 1960 issue of *Sports Illustrated.* Five years earlier, shortly before the Richard Riot, the American magazine had sent the novelist William Faulkner, winner of the 1949 Nobel Prize for Literature, to a Rangers–Canadiens game to report on what he saw. "An Innocent at Rinkside" offered the Mississippi native's reflections on the speed, fluidity, and obscure—to a novice, at least—logic of the sport. Faulkner singled out two Habs for special notice: swift young Bernie Geoffrion and the still-mercurial veteran Maurice Richard. The Rocket, matter of fact, summoned from the novelist the kind of analogy more likely to be found in one of his works of fiction. Richard's relentless motion and perpetual attack mode put William Faulkner in mind of the "glittering fatal alien quality of snakes." Now, assuming his retirement to be pending, *Sports Illustrated* commissioned the artist (and later novelist) Russell Hoban to create a cover image to go along with the piece "Hockey Hero: Montreal's Maurice Richard." The text both commemorated his career and wondered openly how such a man, with such a history, was going to negotiate the inevitable deflation and ordinariness of daily life, post hockey. Hoban's drawing, which could have passed for a century-old woodcut, asked the same question in respectful silence. Showing his head and shoulders only, it depicts Maurice Richard as an aging knight or samurai, his weapon—i.e., his stick—close at hand. Unsmiling and haggard, his expression at once aloof and sad, he stares directly at the reader, a look prideful, unapologetic, and, being so firmly rooted in the value system that has guided him unwaveringly until now, without any inkling of what lies ahead.

CHAPTER SEVEN

Saint Maurice
(of French Canada)

> When it is all over, I'll be a guy like everybody else.
> **MAURICE RICHARD**

In the end, he had to be pushed.

"I've thought about nothing but hockey all my life," he had admitted to the Toronto journalist June Callwood in 1959. "There's a lot I've missed. I don't read books, only magazines on the train. Lots of times I am ashamed because people are talking about things I've never heard about." He loved his children, loved spending time with them, and he certainly loved Lucille, whom he counted on for so much, while admitting that in a marriage "the woman should not be the boss." But Richard, who didn't think he was nearly as good a player as Gordie Howe or Jean Béliveau, or even as his former linemate Elmer Lach, and who had, in his own estimation, achieved what he had for one reason only—"Desire," he said simply—still couldn't conceive of much life beyond the Forum. "Every year I think I ought to get interested in another business, start a restaurant or something. But when the hockey starts I forget about anything else. Maybe if I had other interests, I wouldn't have lasted so long...." His emotions typically exposed, his vulnerabilities drawn out, he added: "I am afraid of the future. I am afraid to grow older. I never used to think on it, now it's on my mind every day. I will be so lonely when hockey is over for me."

Unable to invite that loneliness, Richard delayed and delayed through the summer of 1960. *"C'est le temps que ça change"* ran the campaign slogan of the provincial Liberal Party under Jean Lesage—"Things have to change." Boosted by the unexpected death of Paul Sauvé, Lesage received a mandate from the electorate on June 22. Actually, the Liberals had run their campaign on two slogans, utilizing as well an André Laurendeau–coined expression—*Maîtres chez nous* ("Masters of our own house")—that reflected their determination to implement the spectacular series of reforms and initiatives soon to be bannered as the Quiet Revolution. Maurice Richard surprised many in the media by arriving at the Habs training camp in the Forum in September as usual, overweight and out of shape, either half-believing he might survive another season, despite having missed large parts of the previous three, or else simply needing to have a life change forced upon him. On the second matter, manager Frank Selke obliged. After a scrimmage in which the thirty-nine-year-old scored four goals, Selke called him into his office. He told Richard he was risking serious injury if he kept playing; he also suggested that another partial season with predictably diminished results would tarnish his legacy. Selke offered him a job as team ambassador at his full salary for the first year, and once he received a stunned Richard's terse assent, allowed him no chance to back out, arranging a press conference for that same evening.

Richard went home, numbed, where he explained to Lucille that the Canadiens were forcing him to retire— immediately. Then he dutifully shaved and put on a suit, and drove back to the Queen Elizabeth Hotel on Dorchester Boulevard for a 9 P.M. encounter with print and television media. He spoke in a monotone for five minutes, in both languages, smiled half-heartedly when the journalists gave him a standing ovation, then slipped out a side door. All the reflection and brooding, the attempts to come to terms with the inevitable, were done with; officially, formally, it was over. Maurice Richard, the Rocket, the warrior, the people's hero and avenger, even the diminished but stately elder, had left the building. In his own view, all that remained was just another guy.

BUT HE WAS NO REGULAR *GARS,* and never could be, so long as he lived. At least, so long as he lived in Quebec, where in September 1960 he held the rank of secular saint. It was the highest accolade that could be bestowed on a working-class French Canadian who had endured the Depression and the Great Darkness, and its hallmarks—duty and sacrifice, a passively accepted (if not actively sought) martyrdom particular to the tenets of Catholicism—suited his own sense of honour and obligation. Still, if the agony of his retirement revealed any deeper quality in his nature, it was its resemblance to another solitary figure in society. Hugh MacLennan had called him a "genius." Commentators often used the term "artist" to describe how he played the game. MacLennan was highlighting how instinctive and unselfconscious Richard was as an athlete, and as a growing political force. Those who appreciated him as an artist were suggesting that creativity and self-expression, more than athleticism, set him apart.

A handful of athletes do possess genius IQs, conceptualizing their sport at a higher level than everyone else, and intelligence is always a factor in excellence. Similarly, some are more creative in how they play, and consciously link performance to personality, believing they are expressing themselves as individuals on the court, the field, the ice.

What Maurice Richard displayed in his conversations with journalists, and then in the torturous final year of his career, was something yet more singular. For most players the decision to retire comes down to practical questions and concerns about money, injuries, or a diminishing desire to keep playing. As Richard had admitted, he hadn't really considered these factors. Nor did his manager's offer of a full-time office job with the organization—a courtesy extended to esteemed veterans, granting them a transition period either into management or away from the sport—even register with him. He wasn't a man who had played hockey for a long time, and now had to do something else; he *was* hockey, and almost nothing else. To ask him to stop playing was like asking him to stop being himself. Not to die, exactly, but to be, as he tried to explain to June Callwood, forever after "lonely." He did not mean he would be lonely for his teammates, or for the fans, or necessarily for the sport. He meant that he would be lonely for his own purpose, for a reason for being.

Or for his art? If any quality in Maurice Richard's character made him an artist, it was his wholesale melding of his work with his identity. He could never separate the two, and never wanted to. Out of such an intense, seamless relationship came his extraordinary achievements as a player. But such a relationship is fragile, subject to strains and pressures. With an athlete, it is also at the mercy of time, and less so of place. No matter how he stretched it, Richard's career could not last beyond his fortieth birthday. Nor, given his upbringing and character, and the rare and increasingly complex linkage between his "private" actions on the ice and their "public" import, could it occur elsewhere than in Montreal. Time had now finished him off as a hockey player, which in his mind meant it had finished him off as a man. All he had left to cling to was the place where the Rocket had once lived and worked, and where he would stay on—albeit as just an ordinary private citizen.

He was being both self-abnegating and self-dramatic. As he had been Rocket Richard for the first forty years of his life, now he could be Saint Maurice for the remaining two, three, four decades of it, comfortable among those who revered and appreciated him. He couldn't change, it was true, could no more alter his self-definition than his hairstyle. Happily, over the course of his career it seemed to him that French Canada had barely changed either. But what about that newly elected Liberal Party's slogan: *C'est le temps que ça change?* Amidst his deliberations about retirement and his failing efforts to heal his wounded body, Richard appears not to have registered its import.

THE NEXT FIFTEEN YEARS saw Maurice Richard and Quebec grow more and more apart, until he believed that he had been left behind and forgotten in the only place that mattered to him. Conventional accolades—the retiring of his number by the team, the decision to overrule the normal five-year waiting period and admit him immediately into the Hockey Hall of Fame, his being an inaugural recipient of the Order of Canada—were no consolation. The external reality that he remained the most famous face and name in the province, if not in the entire country, was no greater a source of cheer. He likely couldn't explain why he felt so strongly, or was so bitter, and he certainly couldn't analyze or amend his own behaviour. He was who he was, wise or unwise. Had a friend or, heaven forbid, a psychologist proposed to him that he was actually struggling with the loss of purpose, of the only identity he had known, he would have dismissed the idea as nonsense. Yet Richard, whose professional life had been framed by others, often in the loftiest terms, for some twenty years, now needed to do that framing, that thinking, by himself. Here was another mid-life task that the

Rocket, like most of the tough, no-talk, no-surrender men of his generation, could not begin to undertake.

Predictably, the front-office job with the Canadiens went sour. He was given an office and the title of vice-president, but no real duties or responsibilities. Though the Habs organization would never have admitted it in public, their marquee ex-player was a little rough around the edges to comfortably wear the suit and smile of management. Likewise, from the start Richard felt instinctively uneasy even attempting to play the part of an executive. For other retired star athletes, aware that their employers weren't expecting much from them except the ongoing use of their name and lustre, the impasse would have been fine: extra time to golf, to attend to other projects and enterprises. For Richard, it was an insult. He wanted to be invited to meetings, to be involved in staffing decisions. More importantly, he wanted to help with the direction of the post-dynasty Canadiens, a team that failed to win a Stanley Cup for the first five seasons after he left it—an unacceptable outcome for the franchise renowned for its spring victory parade along the "usual route."

Soon estranged from the team management and the owners, the Molson family, especially after Frank Selke was also forced to retire to make room for newer blood, in 1965

Richard walked away from a salary that, while reduced from the $20,000 he had been paid at the outset, was still decent for what was involved. While he fretted, refusing to allow his name to be associated with the Habs, the squad, now captained by Béliveau and led by his younger brother Henri, returned to its natural winning ways, hoisting four more Cups before the decade ended. The parade along St. Catherine was back on.

Richard missed out on most of that success, rarely attending games, openly brooding about how he had been treated. He turned to various smaller, piecemeal enterprises: speaking engagements and autograph-signing sessions, joining the NHL old-timers' circuit to tour small towns across the country. Those travels provided his first exposure to that vast other Canada, where he was pleasantly surprised to find himself being treated as much as a hockey god as he was in Quebec. He even refereed wrestling bouts. Richard also owned a tavern in Montreal for a few years, an establishment notable both for its refusal to sell Molson's beer and its mixed clientele, and went into the fishing tackle business.

A chance to return to hockey without needing to either swallow his pride or leave the province came in 1972, the year a rival professional league, the World Hockey Association (WHA), was formed. Quebec City was awarded a franchise, called the Nordiques, and they asked Richard to be their head coach, despite his lack of experience running a team. He agreed to lend his prestige to the venture. Nervous and unsure of himself, he lasted exactly two games behind the bench before resigning "for health reasons," a verdict he later admitted was a cover-up for feeling uneasy about being away from his family and Montreal. These mixed business ventures, added to his paltry NHL pension, ensured that Richard could keep his wife and children in middle-class comfort. By 1970, though, his former teammate Jean Béliveau, now also closing in on forty and a step slower than in his prime, was earning over $100,000 with the Habs, as was his own younger brother Henri, still an effective playmaker at age thirty-five. The WHA quickly drove salaries still higher, with Bobby Hull, another player Richard had played against in his twilight years, signing the first-ever million-dollar contract with the Winnipeg Jets.

Soon he would suffer the greater ignominy of watching his one true rival as hockey warrior, Gordie Howe, be lured out of retirement at age forty-four to showcase a small family dynasty in the upstart WHA for the biggest paycheque of his career. The age-defying Howe would go on to play six more seasons, each one a little slower than its predecessor, alongside his sons, Marty and Mark, while the aspirations of Richard's hockey-playing sons, Maurice Jr. and Norman, came to nothing. Howe would even reappear in the NHL at age fifty-one for a curtain call with the Hartford Whalers, in which he still managed to play all eighty regular-season games and score fifteen goals. (He also racked up forty-two penalty minutes, venturing into corners with men three decades his junior, his legendary elbows still high and hard.) His tenacity and fitness, along with all the liberating, financially rewarding recent changes in the sport, meant that Gordie Howe was able to combat the loneliness of retirement for a dozen years longer than Maurice Richard. Here was another tough pill for the Rocket to swallow.

But more than money, more than playing hockey, what Maurice Richard came to miss during his long decade in a largely self-imposed inner exile from the limelight was the Quebec he understood and loved, and which had urgent need of his services. That Quebec, broadly, was the French Canada of the 1940s and '50s, a period of polite, well-groomed athletes in dark suits and fedoras waging nightly battle and bringing home victory for the people; of a dominating, moral-centring Church, with its easy-to-follow rules and obligations; of a solid, stable government, its leader at once a regular "Maurice" and an inscrutable higher entity.

That he could still desire such a society while being increasingly aware, from early adulthood onward, of the injustices rife within it, and even agitate, in his own tentative, anxious manner, for improvements, was not necessarily a sign of a conflicted nature. He wasn't just a man of his times, he was a man who had defined those times. Now, all was changing too rapidly.

Change in Quebec meant change in how Maurice Richard believed he was being remembered. Hubert Aquin's 1962 remark that "You're either Maurice Richard or you're nobody" signalled the onset of a period when the dominant brand of Quebec nationalism had no practical use, and felt some quiet disdain, for Saint Maurice. His attractiveness wasn't enhanced by his known association with the discredited Union Nationale era, that Great Darkness now being abruptly, almost miraculously, lifted. Neither did he endear himself by his ties to both the Catholic Church, in the form of a bestowed sainthood, or even with "French Canada," an identity, perhaps a historical frame, under rapid reconsideration and soon to be abandoned as archaic and pejorative.

He probably wasn't helped either by his literal association, right down to his physical resemblance, with the parents of the young men and women who began to agitate, using the rhetoric of Marxist revolution and the reality of

violent insurrection, during the 1960s. The Front de libéra-
tion du Québec, or FLQ, emerged the same year Aquin
lamented the collective misery of not being Maurice
Richard. By the time of the October 1964 disturbance in
Quebec City, dubbed *samedi de la matraque* or "Saturday of
the Truncheon" by French media for how mounted police
subdued a crowd of demonstrators, the FLQ had been
involved in a year-long terrorist campaign. Bombs were
planted in Westmount mailboxes, on a railway line the
prime minister was scheduled to travel on, and at an army
recruitment centre, the last killing a night watchman. Over
the next six years, cells of the FLQ bombed the Montreal
Stock Exchange and the mayor's residence, robbing banks
to finance their operations. Then in October 1970 the
group kidnapped the British trade commissioner, James
Cross, and the province's labour minister, Pierre Laporte.
Laporte was murdered the day after the imposition of martial law in Montreal. Soldiers and tanks filled the city streets
and hundreds of suspected terrorists and sympathizers were
rounded up by the Quebec provincial police and briefly
interned.

Quebec was shaken by the October Crisis, and the FLQ
fatally discredited. With the demise of revolutionary nationalism went some of its more extreme, disaffected voices,

many from working-class backgrounds, wearers of long hair and bell-bottoms, as much in the thrall of late 1960s youth counterculture as of Karl Marx and Chairman Mao. For this crowd, Maurice Richard held some symbolic connotation as the disgraced hero of the compliant Catholic herd, nothing to celebrate or be especially proud of. But a new kind of nationalist would quickly emerge, largely drawn from the universities and, in the case of its brilliant leader, René Lévesque, print and television journalism. These Quebecers would have no real objection to Saint Maurice.

By the middle of the 1970s, in fact, around the time Richard was being interviewed by the CBC program *The Fifth Estate*, savvy nationalists were starting to appreciate both his historic role and his potential usefulness in the electoral march toward an independent, or at least sovereign, Quebec. With the Canadiens back winning Stanley Cups in the late 1970s—a run of four straight, nearly the match of the glorious 1956–60 reign that he had overseen as captain—there was that much more to link the handsome, dark-haired, well-groomed Maurice Richard with the thickened, silver-haired, sweater-wearing fifty-something-year-old who began to reappear on TV and radio, both as a guest and, once more, as a widely used pitchman for products. The quaint "Saint Maurice" title bothered few; Quebecers had collectively fled the Church the previous decade without any apparent guilt, Catholic or otherwise. But the rest of the honorific—"of French Canada"—needed updating. Quebecers no longer saw themselves as a folkloric society, marginalized and priest-ridden. Instead, they were the *maîtres chez nous* and, on a different level, they believed in *Québec aux Québécois.* Maurice Richard could stay a saint but, if he was to be brought into the secular, confident discussion about the future of the society, he could no longer remain a French Canadian. This fiery *Canadien* and proud *habitant* had to accept a modest title change, a term reflecting what he already was, and had even helped bring into being: *un Québécois.*

CHAPTER EIGHT

Un Québécois

Hey, Rocket, two minutes for looking so good!
GRECIAN FORMULA ADVERTISEMENT, LATE 1970s

"Et maintenant," says the announcer, *"Monsieur Hockey."* March 11, 1996, and the Montreal Forum is celebrating its final night as a hockey shrine. The Canadiens have constructed a new building a few blocks away, below the former Dorchester Boulevard, recently renamed Boulevard René-Lévesque in memory of the late premier. To send off the great arena, their home since 1933, the Habs have invited twenty-two "living legends" onto the ice after the game. One by one they are announced, then step onto the partially carpeted surface to assume a pre-assigned spot. The final player to come out, now a widower and grandfather of fourteen, moves at the pace expected of a seventy-four-year-old. Wearing grey pants, a shirt, and a tie beneath his number 9 Habs jersey, *Monsieur Hockey* walks to his assigned place at

the centre of the triangular arrangement of those legends. Steady applause has greeted Jean Béliveau and Bernie Geoffrion, Guy Lafleur, and Ken Dryden. But for the appearance of Maurice Richard, the crowd of eighteen thousand rises to its feet with the kind of roar usually associated with scoring an overtime goal, and then stays standing, cheering and chanting, for almost eight minutes. There is no question who they're cheering for—the television cameras, picking out the key actors in this drama, rarely pan to the other players, shifting instead between close-ups of Maurice Richard and faces in the crowd—and little question that the ovation is soon more than a tribute to a great athlete. It becomes a performance, a collective assertion. For its spontaneity, its cheerful, flamboyant intensity, the ovation seems as much an acknowledgment of all that Quebec has been through in the previous half-century as of the trials and triumphs of the old man standing on the ice. As he admits later, those eight minutes allow Richard to roll back time in his head, to summon memories and sensations. For those inside the Forum, and watching on television, the minutes become similarly expansive.

0:30. *"Il est perçu comme le symbole de tout un peuple qui se reconnaît dans ses exploits et sa personnalité,"* says Richard Garneau, the Forum announcer associated with so much of the team's glory. His remark, curiously, is not translated by his no-less-esteemed English-language counterpart, broadcaster Dick Irvin Jr., son of Richard's first coach. Were Irvin to translate Garneau, he could explain to younger English-Canadian viewers an essential point about the relationship between Maurice Richard and Quebec, and help them appreciate the monumental event that is unfolding before them: "He is seen as the symbol of an entire nation that recognizes itself in his exploits and in his personality." That symbol has the same groomed hair, now gone grey, and the same dark eyes, watery with age and, increasingly, emotion. He is now a dignified pensioner who endured the loss of his beloved wife to cancer two years earlier. His shy smile and frequent long stares down at the ice, his thick hands once more useless by his sides, suggest the same reticent man, eternally uncomfortable with the attention. By his expression he makes it clear that he both appreciates the ovation and hopes that it will soon end.

1:36. Guessing that he might not be accommodated, Richard turns around and waves to the side of the Forum behind him, then raises his arms partway to ask for calm. Ignoring him, the crowd emits another roar, the volume turned up even higher. He laughs at their response.

2:15. Former teammates and fellow legends Emile Bouchard, seventy-seven, and Elmer Lach, seventy-eight, sensing his discomfort in being under the spotlight for two minutes straight, walk over and lift his arms, like referees declaring a winner in boxing. Richard accepts the boost reluctantly, tries without success to be playful with his old friends, then immediately smoothes his hair after Bouchard ruffles it. The other men, realizing that the light is meant to shine on one person only, quickly withdraw. "Thank you," Richard mouths to the crowd. When they roar still louder, he emits an *"Ah non!"*—closer to his true feelings. No matter: the eighteen thousand former spectators, aware that they are fast making themselves participants in an extraordinary drama, are just getting going.

3:10. Bewildered by the ardour, Richard seems lost in his thoughts. Tears well up, and he rubs his nose to staunch them, dropping his gaze to his feet. He is suddenly exposed and vulnerable, a senior citizen being subjected to almost cruel attention and expectations. But the opposite is actually the case. Another essential truth about his relationship with Quebec is being re-enacted. By abiding almost four minutes of standing ovation, he is doing what he has done since he was a young man: volunteering himself to a cause, accepting that he is part of something larger, and so must bear burdens and fight his own nature. He has always accepted that, when need be, he would play the role of community avenger, secular saint, nationalist icon, statue, name on an arena or trophy, token goodwill ambassador for the Canadiens (a job he resumed in 1991, ending his protracted feud), and, lately, great Québécois, one who has done so much, been put through so much, and emerged—like the society, the province, the people in the Forum that night—with dignity and language, pride and identity, intact. April 1996 is barely six months after the most recent referendum on sovereignty, won narrowly by the federalist side, and Montreal itself is showing signs that it has been through a battle: boarded-up storefronts along St. Catherine Street, *À louer* ("For Rent") signs throughout the downtown. He may not be aware of half this undercurrent and, as always, does not wish to be associated with any political spin. Never in the last quarter-century did Maurice Richard voice public support for sovereignty; never did he seem to view himself as other than a French Canadian, despite outbursts of bitterness toward both Quebec and Canada. But his instinct for the dramatic moment is as unerring now as it was during those playoff runs in the forties and fifties, when he could always be counted on to score the winning goal. He certainly can't be lonely this evening.

Unless, that is, he is thinking of Lucille, who attended every home game and saw him off at Windsor Station for every road trip, and who wasn't only his wife for half a century and mother to their seven children, but by far his best, closest, most faithful friend.

3:43. He tries again to end the applause. If nothing else, it gives him something to do with his hands (the long sweater makes it impossible for him to stuff them in his pockets). Once more, his admirers pay his request no heed.

4:15. *"Mesdames et messieurs ... "* Garneau announces, his own plea for closure. In lieu of quieting down, the crowd starts up a chant last heard with such force in this building in spring 1960: "Rocket! Rocket! Rocket!" On hearing it, Richard pinches his brow and closes his eyes. Later, he admits that the chanting took him back all those decades to when he *was* the Rocket, on that same Forum surface, his inimitable style of play not yet diminished by age and injuries. Images may flash behind his eyelids: goals scored and Cups hoisted, defencemen sidestepped and goalies fooled. Sensations as well: how it felt to move so swiftly, so naturally, that the cold off the surface tickled his cheeks; how muscles, even sore ones, did the mind's bidding, and pain—from a slash across the ankle or wrist, from crashing into the boards shoulder- or even headfirst—was turned into more adrenalin, and deeper desire.

5:02. If he didn't intuit it before, he must now—this ongoing display isn't simply about him. It is about everyone in the building. Whoever wrote the line Garneau read out at the start got it exactly right: French Canadians—or, better, Quebecers, *les Québécois,* a strong, healthy, self-governing people, solidly middle-class, beholden to no *prêtre, patron,* or *chef*—had come to *se reconnaît dans ses exploits et sa personnalité:* to see themselves in his exploits and in his personality. Just as, of course, he had never defined himself as anything other than a working-class French Montrealer, proud and true. TV producers are also coming to recognize the "story" the ovation is trying to tell, and are instructing cameramen to pan more frequently to other players, and to the audience, revealing expressions of astonishment, elation, delight, and great emotion.

5:37. *"Mesdames et messieurs,"* Garneau repeats. A fresh roar, throats now raw and palms sore, once more denies the request. No building announcer is going to shut down *this* celebration. Returning from wherever his thoughts have wandered in the last few minutes, the man who once went on radio and television to ensure that a city would remain calm after a riot he had sparked finally tries again to assert the authority he once commanded with the slightest remark or gesture. "Okay, okay," he mouths, gesturing with his hands. As though meeting him halfway—*non* to ending it, *oui* to a shift in focus—the chant alters from "Rocket!

Rocket!" to the bilingual "Go Habs Go!" Those words are everyday, neither resonant nor magical; the performance is winding down.

7:05. Sensing he now has the upper hand, Garneau issues the closing remark: *"Mesdames et messieurs, vous avez devant vous le coeur et l'âme du Forum"* ("Ladies and gentlemen, you have before you the heart and soul of the Forum"). This time, parallel sentiments are expressed in English. "Ladies and gentlemen," Dick Irvin says, "the Montreal Canadiens Hall-of-Famers." Why so anemic a rendering of so poetic a summation of what has just transpired? Likely, it marks nothing more than differing ad-libs. But the variation feels true to how the languages, the cultures, even the two Canadas, relate to Maurice Richard. As an athlete, a historical figure, he doesn't belong exclusively to Quebec, or to French Canadians. Far from it. But as a man, his *coeur* and his *âme* certainly do, and everything he has done and said in his seventy-four years has emerged from those allegiances, that identity.

FOUR YEARS AND ONE MONTH later again, Richard, having succumbed to abdominal cancer, will dominate the ice used by the Montreal Canadiens for a final time, his body lying in state in the new arena for a day while some 115,000 people pay their respects. At the family's request, the casket will not be draped in the fleur-de-lys, to avoid politicizing the funeral, and among the 2,700 who attend the service at Notre-Dame Basilica will be Governor General Adrienne Clarkson, Prime Minister Jean Chrétien, and sovereignist premier Lucien Bouchard. Also in attendance will be most of those same "living legends," along with Gordie Howe, who flies in from Michigan, where he lives in retirement. Tens of thousands more Montrealers will line St. Catherine Street, traditional route of the now-infrequent Stanley Cup parades, shouting "Maurice! Maurice!" as the cortège goes past. That event will be dignified and fitting, but it will be no match for the spontaneity and surprise, the unscripted delight, of the 1996 Forum ovation for Maurice Richard, a moment of transcendent, joyful noise.

Barbottes

It was the ugliest thing I had ever seen. *Mon oncle* René called it *une barbotte,* and said it was good eating; *mon oncle* Aurèle translated for me. Catfish, he said in English of the flat-headed fish with whiskers spiking out its cheeks and chin, and wait'll you hear 'em squeal. I was thirteen, one of Muriel's kids, meaning I hadn't been raised bilingual in the town or in Espanola. My brother and sister and I were from down south, Toronto; we spoke only English. René Lacroix, my godfather, worked at the mill and smoked Craven A and drank beer and rye. I adored him. Aurèle Bruno did pretty much the same, and I adored him as well. We were out on the Blind River catching ugly fat catfish, bottom-feeders who bit on any lure and seemed to jump into the boat without needing to be tricked, and talking about this and that. With me, *mes oncles* spoke English, clear but accented; with each other, *le français,* nasally and singsong, as my mother did with her sisters. We mostly talked about the Habs, who'd won the Cup again that spring, after losing the previous season to the Bruins, which had been bad, though not as *épouvantable* as back in '67, when they'd lost to the Leafs, which remained *calice* and *maudit tabernacle*—whatever those words meant—six years later. My uncles, I could tell, didn't believe it when I said I wasn't a Leafs fan. I was from there, after all; I was half them, kind of, though they knew my dad was of Ottawa Irish stock, and hunted and fished like a real *Canadien*, and had been working in the bush staking claims in 1953 when he met the second-youngest Fallu girl in Blind River, and married her.

No, I kept saying while the buckets kept filling with slimy *barbottes*, I cheer for Montreal. Jean Béliveau remained my hero—I had a poster of him on my bedroom door—even though he had retired two years earlier. And goalie Rogatien Vachon had been a favourite (I played goal as well) until they traded him to the Kings. But Yvan Cournoyer and Jacques Lemaire, Guy Lafleur and the Mahovlich brothers were all fantastic. I even liked the ancient team captain, Henri "Pocket Rocket" Richard, though he sure moved slowly out there.

And the Rocket himself, *mon oncle* René asked, raising an eyebrow. You like the Rocket?

I knew about Henri's legendary older brother, of course, but had never seen him play. There was a family story about

Maurice Richard: how my Aunt Anna and Uncle Ernie had named their boys after him—Maurice, born in '50, and Richard, born in '52. Poor little Richard was sick from birth, and died when he was seven. The Rocket learned somehow about the brothers who shared his names and that one was fighting cancer, and tried visiting them when he was in Sudbury. (Everyone knew he loved kids.) He ran out of time, and so sent along signed photos instead: "To Maurice, from Maurice Richard," and "To Richard, from Maurice Richard." Fourteen years later, the family still spoke about his generosity, if not so much about the boy who died.

He stopped playing the year I was born, I said.

There was no one like the Rocket, my godfather said. Not then, not now. Not never.

The Mahovlich boys are from up here, said *mon oncle* Aurèle. He talked too fast in English and had too few teeth. Timmins way, he added.

Are they French? I said.

Could be. Should be, he said.

As a small child I'd known this: drive north out of our Toronto suburb for eight or nine hours, stopping in Sudbury to visit *ma tante* Anna and her (living) children Maurice and Louise, and people, or family at least, started saying things in French and being French Canadians. But at school I'd learned differently: French was spoken in the part of the country well east of Toronto, in the province of Quebec, where everyone was Québécois and *le bleu, blanc, rouge* played the best hockey in the world. But my mother's family, my dozen *tantes* and *oncles* and my dozens and dozens of *cousins,* all Habs fanatics who watched the French telecasts on Saturday nights, cheering and cursing in French, lived in Ontario. The cousins around my age had softer accents and bigger English vocabularies than their parents. They were also more curious about down south. They wanted to go to college in Toronto, find a job there, play their songs in bars and see bands at Maple Leaf Gardens. They were nervous about the city—the dangers, the expense, how people would look at them, treat them—but they were going anyway: to get out of the north, out of a town with one block of stores and one theatre and one industry, the mill, rumoured to be going bankrupt any day now. Later I learned that my mother's family were officially designated as Franco-Ontarians, and as French-speakers they were tiny and vulnerable, at risk of vanishing through assimilation. Outside an independent Quebec, some believed, they didn't stand a chance. "Still-warm corpses," the nationalist author Yves Beauchemin would famously call them, inaccurately.

That July afternoon in 1973, we docked the boat, transferred three pails brimming with catfish to the car, and drove two minutes to the Lacroix house. René and my godmother, *ma tante* Marie, lived in a tiny house with a front door but no steps leading up to it, and a side door that everyone used. During our summer and holiday visits I sometimes slept in the dormer room above the kitchen. I adored *ma tante* Marie most of all, for her tourtières and apple pies and for how kindly she looked at me. Family and visitors always sat in the kitchen, smoking, drinking, eating, and if there were just a couple of *tantes* and *oncles,* they usually remembered to speak English for my dad, and us kids. But if more showed up—Tante Lucille, Tante Del, Tante Rita, Tante Hélène, Tante Pauline, all lived in town, with more *tantes* in other towns, and one, a nun named Soeur Cécille, over in Rome, working for the Pope—they forgot and slid back into French. Today, there was Lucille and Aurèle, René and Marie, Dave and Muriel. Tante Marie asked if I wanted to help cook. I said yes, not because I did, but because she asked. Off the back of the kitchen was a narrow room with a laundry sink. I transferred the *barbottes* from the pails into the sink, trying not to be grossed out by their calf-smooth skin, and then watched as *mon oncle* whacked each one between the eyes with the blunt end of an axe. He wore his bifocals and dangled a Craven A from his lips.

The fish did make sounds. I didn't hear the squeals my other uncle had warned me about; I heard the squeak of a rusty door hinge, the grinding of bones in a shoulder socket, and then, unmistakably—to my ears—the whimpers of a creature knowing it was being exterminated, and not knowing why. *Barbottes,* I found out, bled when they were carved up, drenching the counter. Their heads, even after being separated from their bodies, kept going for a few minutes longer, mouths opening and closing, whiskers twitching. Their eyes, mercifully, showed no residue of life.

Retreating, I slumped into a table chair. Marie and Lucille were dipping strips of fish in milk and rolling them in flour and salt, laying them in frying pans a half-inch deep in cooking oil. The kitchen soon broiled, the air dense with cigarette smoke and my father's pipe, the raw stink of a catfish fry. Sitting there, a little woozy but also happy—I was always happy in Blind River—I thought back to the conversation in the boat. Why had I been rooting for the Montreal Canadiens for as long as I could remember? Why did I pay closer attention to *Hockey Night in Canada* interviews with French players than ones with English guys on the Leafs, or the Bruins, or the Red Wings? Listening, looking, listening, looking, it came clear to me: *mes oncles* not only talked English like Guy Lafleur and Jacques Lemaire, they smiled and frowned, moved their hands and combed their hair, as did Henri Richard and Jean Béliveau. And though I knew him mostly just as a famous face and a family story, my handsome uncles all somehow looked like, and, I bet, sounded like, the Rocket—like Maurice Richard. They were like him, and I—well, half of me—was like them, him, in return. This was who I was, even if I couldn't speak the language very well and lived in Toronto. *Ma famille pour toujours.*

SOURCES AND ACKNOWLEDGMENTS

Maurice Richard lives on in various forms and media. I consulted the CBC and Radio-Canada websites for their television and radio clips from his playing days and after, and found extraordinary material, including versions of the ovation described in Chapter 7, on YouTube. In keeping with our accelerated age, more and more material will shortly come online—a bonus for future historians and biographers. I examined Charles Binamé's 2005 film *The Rocket* for its fine period detail, including its recreations of dramatic events from a career that partially predated television, as well as for Roy Dupuis's insightful performance as Richard. I also watched with great pleasure the ten-part CBC television series *Hockey: A People's History*. Adrienne Clarkson first remembered *The Fifth Estate* documentary "The Rocket at 54," and suggested I track it down; Sally Reardon at the program found it and kindly sent me a copy; Brian McKenna, who directed the segment, generously offered recollections of filming and interviewing Maurice Richard.

First and foremost among book sources is *The Rocket: A Cultural History of Maurice Richard* (Vancouver: Greystone Books, 2009) by Benoît Melançon. Melançon, a professor of literature at the Université de Montréal, examines Richard from a variety of cultural perspectives. The result is an exploration as unique to Canadian culture as, perhaps, Richard was to Canadian hockey. I am in particular debt to Melançon for his striking meditation on Saint Sebastian and Saint Maurice. I read *The Rocket* in its elegant translation by Fred A. Reed, and made use of his renderings of Quebec song lyrics and plays. Roch Carrier's *Our Life with the Rocket: The Maurice Richard Story* (Toronto: Penguin Canada, 2001, translated by Sheila Fischman) was another valuable resource, as was Jean-Marie Pellerin's *Maurice Richard: L'idole d'un peuple* (Montreal: Les Éditions de L'Homme, 1976). *Remembering the Rocket: A Celebration* (Toronto: Stoddart Publishing, 1998), edited by Craig MacInnis, contains wonderful reportage from the era, including Hugh MacLennan's 1955 foray into the other solitude, "The Rocket: A Hero for Quebec," and two profiles by June Callwood. D'Arcy Jenish's *The Montreal Canadiens: 100 Years of Glory* (Toronto: Doubleday Canada, 2008) and *Lions in Winter* (Toronto: McGraw-Hill Ryerson, 1994) by Chrys Goyens and Allan Turowetz are both authoritative accounts of the franchise, and I learned about the darker side of the sport from *Net Worth: Exploring the Myths of Pro Hockey* (Toronto: Penguin Books, 1991), the groundbreaking exposé by David Cruise and Alison Griffiths. Michael McKinley's *Putting a Roof on Winter: Hockey's Rise from Sport to Spectacle* (Vancouver: Greystone Books, 2000) is an excellent history of shinny from its earliest days, and David

Zirin's *What's My Name, Fool?: Sports and Resistance in the United States* (Chicago: Haymarket Books, 2005) helped inform my thinking about the class dimensions to Maurice Richard's career and life.

My thinking was, needless to say, also informed and frequently reformed by conversations about Richard and Quebec. For their time and patience I am especially grateful to Henri Richard, Dick Irvin Jr., Dave Stubbs, Mark Abley, Dr. Bryan Palmer, Dr. Brian J. Young, Frank McArdle, and Roy McMurtry. Adam Gopnik, Michael Levine, and Jackie Kaiser are owed general thanks, as is Paul Piché, for permission to quote from his song "Essaye donc pas." Andrew Cohen read a draft of *Maurice Richard* and provided superb notes, and Diane Turbide and Scott Steedman applied their editorial acumen to the manuscript. Finally, the book emerged from a series of conversations between myself and John Ralston Saul, and with each exchange my arguments grew stronger and clearer. I am deeply thankful to John for his support and his vigorous and expansive edit.

1921	Joseph Henri Maurice Richard is born on August 4 in Montreal.
1925	He receives his first set of skates.
1935	He plays his first organized hockey games for his home parish of Bordeaux.
1937	Richard quits high school to help his family by training as a machinist.
1938	He meets Lucille Norchet, the sister of a teammate.
1939	He scores 133 of his team's 144 goals; tries out for junior squad, the Verdun Maple Leafs.
1940	Richard moves up inside the Canadiens organization; breaks his ankle after one game.
1941	He misses much of the season with a broken wrist.
1942	He marries Lucille Norchet; makes the Canadiens team, but breaks his leg in December.

1943   Richard attempts to enlist in the Canadian army for combat duty, but fails the physical due to damage to his femur, ankle, and wrist. He switches to number 9 in honour of the birth weight of his first child, Huguette.

1944   He rejoins the Canadiens squad; earns the nickname "The Rocket." Canadiens win Stanley Cup.

1944   He's turned down by the Canadian military for the third time.

1944–45   He scores fifty goals in fifty games.

1945   Conn Smythe, owner of Toronto Maple Leafs, attempts to buy Richard for $25,000.

1945–55   Six more children are born to Maurice and Lucille: Maurice Jr., Norman, André, Suzanne, Polo, and Jean.

1946   The Habs win the Stanley Cup again.

1947   Richard wins his only Hart Trophy for outstanding player. He holds out for a pay raise in the autumn, without success.

1948   His valued linemate Toe Blake suffers a career-ending injury. The Canadiens struggle.

1951   Richard becomes Montreal's all-time leading scorer. The team reaches the first of ten successive finals, but doesn't win.

1952   Richard scores a famous playoff goal against "Sugar" Jim Henry.

1953   Montreal finally signs Jean Béliveau to the team. They lose in the finals to Detroit.

1954   Richard uses his newspaper column to criticize NHL president Clarence Campbell.

1954–55   He gives up the column under pressure; records the highest penalty total of his career.

1955   March 13: Richard pummels a Boston player with his stick, repeatedly, then attacks a linesman.

              March 16: Campbell suspends Maurice Richard for the remainder of the season and the entire playoffs.

              March 17: The "Richard Riot" erupts inside the Forum and along St. Catherine Street.

1956–60   Canadiens win five straight Stanley Cups with an older, mellower Richard.

1957	He scores his five-hundredth goal on October 19.
1957–60	Richard serves as team captain.
1958–60	His regular-season play is limited by injuries.
1960	Richard is forced to retire; accepts position with team management.
1965	He resigns from the Canadiens organization.
1967	Richard is inducted into the Order of Canada.
1972	He briefly coaches the Quebec Nordiques of the WHA.
1975	Richard appears in a CBC *The Fifth Estate* documentary.
1991	He resumes working for the Canadiens as a goodwill ambassador.
1994	Lucille Richard dies of cancer.
1996	Farewell ovation for Richard, and for the Forum, on March 11.
1999	The trophy for the NHL scoring leader is renamed for Richard.
2000	Maurice Richard dies of cancer, age 78, on May 27.

—— COLLECT THEM ALL ——

— COLLECT THEM ALL —

René Lévesque
by DANIEL POLIQUIN

Nellie McClung
by CHARLOTTE GRAY

Marshall McLuhan
by DOUGLAS COUPLAND

L.M. Montgomery
by JANE URQUHART

Lester B. Pearson
by ANDREW COHEN

Maurice Richard
by CHARLES FORAN

Mordecai Richler
by M.G. VASSANJI

Louis Riel &
Gabriel Dumont
by JOSEPH BOYDEN

Pierre Elliott Trudeau
by NINO RICCI

EXTRAORDINARY
CANADIANS

Why They Mattered Then.
Why They Matter Now.